The Sentient Struggle for Transformation

Whickwithy

"Education of the mind without education of the heart is no education at all"
  -Aristotle

The Sentient Struggle for Transformation

All rights reserved

ISBN: 978-1-7348221-4-4   Mature audiences only

The Sentient Struggle for Transformation by Whickwithy

First Edition End of 2022

Previous efforts:
Sentience
A Sentient Perspective
Beauty & Fiction
Millennium
Book 6

Infini Entendre
   (Infini Entendre is poetry, very little of it applies directly to the grand scheme of our humanity, but all of it applies indirectly)

   If you desire to read further, after this book, I would suggest skipping *Beauty & Fiction* and *Book 6*. They seem redundant.

The Sentient Struggle

If humanity matches its intellect with emotional stability, we will have created an unstoppable force. Our sentience awaits us.

We started out as little more than animals many thousands of years ago. Over that vast span, the animal has kept dragging us back to its limitations. The animal has been witlessly in charge.

One situation was just far too confusing for our ancestors.

For more than three thousand years we have been struggling, stumbling towards our sentience. It has been a stumbling effort because we have never really known what sentience entails. We keep convincing ourselves that we were no more than an animal.

We have tried to convince ourselves that we are human. We are not yet. All because of a single lie.

We used our intelligence to build laws and civilization to restrain the animal within us. That was our intelligence at work.

Intelligence is only the halfway house to a sentient state. Laws and culture only restrain the animal. It does not make us human. The animal still rules and shows itself at the drop of a hat. Only our full, unobstructed awareness can rid us of the delusions of the animal in order to become human.

Sentient awareness and education of the heart make us human. We have refuted what our sentience awareness tells us. That has corrupted our heart. Love is more than just words.

As long as the most common description of our prehuman state is, "We're _only_ human", we are not. Do you even hear the defeatist attitude in that statement? The human will hear it.

When we can finally say with sincerity, "Omigosh! We are _human_!!!", we will be. It will be an incredible accomplishment.

For the last three thousand years, we have never made a serious attempt to attain our humanity. We have only picked away at the animal hidden in the shadows, making laws to tell the animal what to do, avoiding the issue that leaves us nothing more than a demented animal.

Our past has mostly been comprised of the animal overdoing what it has always done: whatever it desires with only the slightest thought in its head. It has been an emotional upheaval as never before seen. It is not human. It is not animal. It is somewhere in between.

Humanity requires balance. The heart, as well as the mind, needs to be educated. The heart's education is missing. Emotional stability is missing. We hide from our sentience state.

Our past has not been human. It has been an overly intelligent animal reveling in its newly born, heightened intellect, never suspecting that there is far more to sentient life than a witless run amok. Sentient awareness has not been released.

The quiet struggle to attain our sentient state has been a subtle movement that has been all but unapparent. Because it has been in the shadows, because we could never look our failure in the eye, in order to attain a sentient state, our image of what humanity can be, what our potential really is, has been diminished, downplayed beyond measure.

Amidst all of the clamor and din of seeking our sentience, while reveling and destroying all in our path and misinterpreting so much our existence, we have slowly and quietly uncovered what is really going on. The pieces have slowly been put together in the background over the span of millennia but, mostly, over the last two hundred years. The blinders are gone.

Pieces Of The Puzzle

For thousands of years we have had nearly all of the pieces of the puzzle and, yet, because of a single missing piece, we have never been able to put it all together to become more than a demented animal. One single piece of the puzzle has continually defeated our sentient awareness.

One piece of the puzzle that has been available for all those long years are the noble human characteristics. We *know* these characteristics. They should easily be attained. Yet, the finer qualities are rare indeed and becoming rarer by the moment. All because the maniacal animal remains unchanged and utterly in charge. All because we could not face a single truth.

Honour, dignity, integrity, honesty, caring, compassion, empathy, generosity of spirit, responsibility, grace, joy, the celebration of life, et al are seldom experienced. Deftness, finesse, ingenuity, flair, creativity, agility, adroitness, resourcefulness are often missing from the scene.

How can it be that the we have always known about these human traits but never fulfilled them? What kept us blinded, unable to adopt the traits that are so clearly human? *For three thousand years*, we have been spinning our wheels in confusion. We remain in a prehuman state in which the cruel animal rules. The noble characteristics have been mostly forgotten, set aside.

We are still no more than an animal *acting out* the part of the human, while remaining essentially an animal. We are a bit smarter than the animal. That has only made us demented. It all remains an act. The elusive answer to our sentient state remains beyond our comprehension. The answer is at our fingertips. Honest sentient awareness knows what is going on.

Shakespeare put it so well. It has been a tale told by an idiot, full of sound and fury, signifying nothing. No one has taken the time to realize why that remains true. We just accept it, never expecting it to change. We accept humanity as a genetically inherent idiot. That is ridiculous. It is the stupour of the animal.

It has never made a bit of sense. Why does it continue to remain that way? We continue on like an animal, even though we know better. Our sentient awareness has been crushed. The forced stupour has acted as stand-in.

All because one piece confounded us. There is one, crucial missing piece of the puzzle. We avoid peering into our humanity because the animal made the rules by which we live and love, long before awareness began to take center stage. We have been confounded. It has been a battle for sentient liberation.

A Sentient Reality

There is little difference between the neanderthal and the bespoke man with a briefcase walking down main street. We are still, in almost every way, little more than an animal. Only our intellect differentiates us from the animal. That is not enough. Without the balance provided by accepting that which our sentient awareness makes clear, we remain deranged. Without education of the heart, we remain a demented animal.

We are aware of so much more than any animal, *whether we like it or not*. *That* is crucial. We cannot avoid our awareness.

The disruption to our existence is due to one incongruity that our sentient awareness made apparent that dates back to before humanity ever existed. We severely blocked it from our sentient awareness with deceits, delusions, and confusion long before we could articulate the issue in a human manner. The animal created a rampant coverup. The subconscious is the repository for that which we have failed to confront. While our intellect was unaffected, our sentient awareness was forced into a stupour.

We can cast off the animal, decisively and irrevocably, in an virtual heartbeat. Our sentience has been aware of the answer all along. We ran and hid from an aspect of the animal's existence that doesn't make sense for a human.

Long ago, like a befuddled animal, we could not cope. Then, we buried the crucial awareness so deep it has taken us millennia to excavate. Once we accept what it has been telling us, we become human. We will know when we are human when we no longer revert to the animal at the drop of a hat.

The demented state of humanity that you see all around you began long ago. It has been compounded, generation after generation, ever since. The clutter of delusional animal paradigms makes us afraid to peer into the unknown for fear of what we may find. The animal and the stupour rule.

The irony of the ages is that we have been hiding from that which fulfills our humanity, our sentience, and creates a beneficent existence. It will not be a utopia but far better than the awful dystopia that we have endured for millennia.

All due to a single instance of the animal's fear of the unknown that was too much for an ancient ancestors. We shut down our thought processes, our sentient awareness, and left our humanity undone. All because our befuddled ancient ancestors were much closer to the animal than the human. All because the animal's fear of the unknown was upon us.

Sentient Awareness

Conscious awareness began in earnest with verbalization, articulation, and shared elucidation. That brought most topics out of the subconscious. We began to question, seek answers, share insights, and make changes to suit what had been revealed by our heightened awareness. Like no animal before us.

One subject became off-limits, verboten, taboo. We wouldn't even think about it, much less mention it, because we were at a loss as to how to rectify it. It was broken and we knew it. In desperation, we shut down our conscious awareness on that one crucial topic. By doing so, we shut down our sentient awareness and that which makes us human. We have stumbled along blindly for more than three millennia.

Once we comprehend a situation, allow it into our conscious awareness, we can adjust it to conform to our desires. Because of a misinterpretation of circumstances, we slowly shut down our sentient awareness on one particular subject, for fear of what we may find. The fear, lying, and loathing took over. We allowed the animal's stupour to rule instead of conscious awareness.

An awful compulsion has driven us since the beginning. The convolutions within convolutions within convolutions that we have created wrench the mind. Our twisted past has nearly broken us. Coherent thought has been cut off at the knees. Conscious awareness has been undermined.

Our first foray into sentience ended before it ever began. We never faced what our sentience has been telling us all along regarding the difference that makes us human.

Our sentient awareness will never let it go. It can't. It is the *truth*. The root cause of our troubles is a failure that we can *never* accept. It has haunted us since the beginning. Our ancestors buried the most significant treasure of our humanity beneath so much flotsam it has taken us millennia to unearth.

We have run roughshod over our existence. We blinded ourselves to a simple failure that preceded us. We lied to ourselves on a grand scale due to a single subject. We never acknowledged it. We acted like it didn't exist. If it was good enough for animals, dammit, it was good enough for humanity.

We remain confounded, deceived, demented, and delusional three thousand years after our sentient awareness first attempted to emerge. All due to a single subject that we would not consider. The remnants of what should be coherent thought have produced a train wreck. Look around. It is an animal's reign.

The basis for reality

In its most essential form, the basis for reality is truth and honesty. Sentience is always seeking truth. Even truths that an animal could never deal with. Sentience attempts to correlate what it senses with what it understands of existence. We broke from reality long ago because of an issue that we would not face. We became liars. Our sentient awareness never ceases to attempt to make the truth apparent. Sentience is always an honest effort.

We are not natural-born liars. Sentience *always* attempts to provide honest perceptions that correlate to the circumstances it encounters. Our sentience is relentless. In the face of the lies that we propound, it drives us mad. An honest portrayal of circumstances is our most precious gift and requirement.

As a demented sentient race, we 'interpret' reality as if it were a plaything to be manipulated. The beast took advantage of the of our heightened creativity and imagination in order to hide something from us. It has run rampant ever since. Thus, we became a demented animal.

'Perception is reality' is a befuddled animal's take on existence. The foolish concept of interpreting reality (i.e. lying) was initiated by the unmooring of our sentience long ago.

A single aspect of the animal's existence did not correlate with our sentient perceptions of what reality entails for a human. Our ancestors couldn't face the inconsistency that our sentience revealed. They ignored what our sentience questioned. They tore our sentient reality to pieces rather than accept that there was something about an animal's situation that did not suit us.

Our ancient ancestors could not easily overturn, therefore never admitted, a certain predicament of the animal that is not suitable to a thinking human. The misfire had been ongoing for a billion years before humanity ever existed. It was such a 'natural' occurrence that it was never openly questioned.

We would not mention it. We would not even think about it. Because of the delusions and deceits, we have crashed through our existence for three millennia as we followed in the footsteps of the animal. The initial lie perverted everything.

The initial lie has proliferated throughout every aspect of our existence, leaving nothing untouched. Coherent thought was was lost in the stupour. Lies took its place. We created babble and gibberish to substitute for our sentient awareness.

We are quickly approaching the pinnacle of our stupour. Just look around. It is all around you. Everyone has their own version of a pseudo-reality that is nothing more than a concoction of misery, lies, confusion, and delusion. The lies are dripping from our tongues. The veil of tears is not for humanity.

Root cause

While the big picture is far more complex than I initially comprehended, the root cause of our troubles remains the same. The basis for a sentient reality remains elusive, lost amidst the distortions, confusion, and fear of the animal.

Animals can't change. They are too dim-witted. For a billion years, a certain aspect of animal life remained unchanged. The change is not only beyond them. It would be disastrous for a dim-witted animal to make such a change. They accept life as it is given to them. That is as it should be - for an animal.

The discrepancy between the animal's situation and what we perceive as the truth, what we *know* is true, left us lost.

Emotional stability has never existed. The heart has never been educated. The missing piece of the puzzle provides for the emotional integrity that is required to stabilize our heightened human intellect and liberate our sentient awareness from its subconscious cage and the lies we tell ourselves.

Masters Of Themselves

Men like to think of themselves as Masters Of The Universe. Male sentient awareness knows better. There is something that compromises the male human. His ability to give is undermined.

The "Masters Of The Universe" *act* is nothing but a horrible facade, an *act* to hide a deep wound in men that has never gone away and never been admitted. Men are not in charge of their own emotions, much less their actions because of it.

The animal buried the wound with prejudice.

We have erroneously convinced ourselves that the disruptive behaviour of the male gender is genetic or, somehow, a mysterious, aspect of the male human. It is only the befuddled remains of the animal that has not learned to give.

The tale told by an idiot, full of sound and fury, signifying nothing is only caused by the tattered remnants of the male animal that need not remain. The tale told by an idiot can end.

Forget the universe, men need only become masters of themselves.

The Ongoing Love Experiment

Approximately seventy years ago, there was a generation that was termed the 'Free Love' or Flower Power generation. It was our sentient awareness hard at work, once again, attempting to free our consciousness by forcing us to admit the truth.

They never achieved 'free love', though that was the goal. They were young. No one had told them that free sex did not equate to free love. Sex became without restrictions. The animal won again. The male still never learned to give.

That generation unlocked the mysterious link between sex and love that our sentience awareness has always known, but we have avoided at all costs for three millennia due to fear.

While that generation failed to reveal the basis for a sentient reality, they blew the doors wide open regarding sex. The Flower Power generation essentially, inadvertently, and unexpectedly exposed the sham that humanity has bought for millennia. It still didn't take because the experience of love remained vague, as it does to this day.

The thought that made every generation shudder and quake was finally upon us. The answer remained hazy but it was clear enough. The two concepts, love and sex, were indelibly linked.

Since the link was in view but still unattained, humanity went looking to liberate it. The link remained undefined, caged in our subconscious. The baton was passed on. The truth shall out.

The LGBTQ movement knew the answer. *Loving* sex is all about *mutual* orgasm. The link between sex and love was finally established. LGBTQ saw through what, the mostly heterosexual, Flower Power generation could never admit openly. The Flower Power generation had opened Pandora's Box ... for the last time.

Love begins with mutual orgasm. For love to flourish, it *requires* mutual orgasm. Love is initiated with loving sex. A loving existence relies on love's physical component.

The transcendent experience of orgasm is not just for men. Because of the conditioning of the ages, we convinced ourselves that loving coitus was impossible. That forced us to convince ourselves to never broach the subject of mutual orgasm *for three thousand years. Wrong on both counts.* Disaster dressed up as sanctity. Love has taken a beating ever since.

Men have remained inhibited, less than a human, because of an incongruity of animal sex that has never been accepted for the failure that it is, understood, or overcome. Male animals take and female animals give. Men can learn to give and, thus, become human.

It begins in bed. It balances humanity. It educates the heart.

The LGBTQ movement blew the doors wide open on *love*.

Women have given and given and given throughout the ages.

Spoiler alert:

Mutual coital (i.e. heterosexual) orgasm can become the common result, even though it has taken us millennia. Our dull-witted ancient ancestors set us on a false trail long, long ago.

Today, it is closer to one in ten or a hundred men that can provide for mutual orgasm during unassisted coitus. That can change. The tale told by an idiot can end.

The compromised ability of men to give starts in bed. That can end. Men can give during coitus. Men *cannot* learn to give until they learn to love. It is so simple, it is embarrassing.

Men can easily last as long as *she* desires. It has always been an *unnecessary, blind* failure. It is easy to overcome what an animal never could for a billion years. We are human. We think.

It seemed intimidating that animals consistently failed to make coitus an act of mutual orgasm *for a billion years*. Forget the numbers, forget the years. Just remember: we are human.

We think. The one confounding aspect of the problem was our fear of failure and forced blindness to the problem. All we ever needed to do was rid ourselves of the fear, face this issue squarely, and reorient our thinking. Instead, we measured the common result and threw up our hands. Three minutes became the goal. Let's be clear: the goal is as long as *she* desires.

Be reassured. Nature provided for the fulfillment of a sentient race's desire for loving coitus. I mean, duh!

But, more importantly, under any conditions, we must accept the situation and deal with it. We have to quit lying to ourselves. Rutting is not love. Mutual orgasm is required in order to become human and loving, however it is done. Nature provided.

We have followed the nonsense of our ancestors without ever questioning their most basic assumptions. Men have continued to fail at loving coitus *only* because we accepted a single ancient assumption of the animal: men are on a clock as soon as they penetrate. Nothing could be further from the truth.

Male animals are on a clock. We are not just an animal. We can put aside the clock. We think. It makes us human. We can overcome the instincts that cause coitus to end abruptly in failure. We are not a stupoured animal, even though we still act out the part. There is no other word for it. Lack of mutual orgasm is failure. This is all explained in detail in Details.

Though men have tried continually, the utter nonsense, along with the fear of delving deeper, derailed the effort. Both of which were passed down, generation to generation.

This is the shame that men have erroneously, inadvertently, offensively, witlessly, and wrongly been hiding from for three thousand years. The concealment has destroyed our humanity.

If men had ever faced the situation openly, they would have realized that there was never any need for shame and certainly no need for failure. The only shame is hiding from the problem.

Before our sentience could really take control, the animal, at a loss, went to work to create fear and denial in order to hide from the issue. Once we look the issue squarely in the eye, we are free. Even better, once resolved it, we will liberate our humanity.

The issue that men fear is easily resolved - *for a human*. Nature provided. We just weren't paying attention. See Details.

The incongruity of it all is stupefying. However it is done, a couple deserves to experience mutual orgasm. We have tried desperately to hide from the fact that giving in bed is paramount for love to exist between a couple. Because of that, we remained an animal, a demented one at that. All because coitus has not been able to provide love consistently. Hiding from truth has the most abhorrent, ludicrous effect on our sentient state.

Worse yet, it was plain stupid. Our instilled fear of failure is the only reason that we failed to make coitus work as it should for a human. Nature provided everything required. We did not use our wit, until now, to realize it. It is all in Details.

It makes me want to punch something.

When is humanity going to admit that something is fundamentally wrong? Why has it taken us so long to observe the fact that there is a source for our troubles? It is so much more than random aberrancies of individuals?

In other words, we are not human yet. I know the answer thoroughly because I delved where no other dared to look. No one else could bear the brunt of facing our awful situation.

When will we realize that we have never educated the heart? When will we realize that we are not fully sentient yet?

We accepted a lie long, long ago because the truth was too much to bear *for our ancient ancestors* that were dumber than a bag of hammers. We have accepted the answer of an animal *for three millennia* because our early ancestors were closer to an animal than a human. They had no knowledge and little wit.

Not only did they bury the answer but also the question. As long as the lie is accepted and the truth remains lurking in the subconscious, we remain nothing more than a demented animal.

When traced back, there is a single source for all of the animal's antics that we endure daily. It has been hiding among us all along. We still attempt to blame individual actions rather than the lie that affects us all in different ways. None of them good.

Our ancient ancestors accepted and buried the truth about a single subject because they could not contend with the question.

We accept a ludicrous version of sentience because those ancient ancestors buried the joker so far beneath fear and loathing that we have been stumbling along ever since, never even admitting to the question, much less facing the answer.

Our descendants will probably have a good laugh over the ridiculous predicament of their immediate ancestors. The irony of it all is unprecedented. SMH

I am not laughing now.

We can educate the heart by overturning one lie.

The lie is simple and everyone grows up with it: coitus is a wonderful experience. It can be. It isn't now.

Coitus is a disappointment and nobody wants to admit it. No one is truly satisfied with the way coitus works for an animal but we have been all too ashamed to say so.

Neither man nor woman likes the fact that coitus is incomplete. Those that find some other way to achieve mutual orgasm alleviate the situation for themselves by side-stepping the issue at hand. That is far better than the lie we have all accepted.

Sure, coitus makes babies. What else could we ask for?

We could ask for honesty. We could ask for human intervention. We could ask to, at least, admit the situation instead of hiding from it.

As you will see, I have delineated how to make coitus a loving, *human* experience. Even without that, though, it is crucial that we at least *quit lying to ourselves!* The fears are many. "What if everyone admitted that coitus is not fulfilling to a sentient being *and why. Maybe we'd stopped doing it!?!*"

They are ludicrous fears because the real issue has never been faced, much less uttered, as we remain dumbfounded. We rely on people that don't even have sex to tell us that sex is just for making babies. The concocted stories with religious overtones, from our distant past induce the fear that keeps us from openly observing what is really going on. Pompous mouths spew lies of the animal. Like The Garden Of Eden, that blames women for our ills, to turn us away from delving into the real problem.

What really happens once we admit the truth? We deal with it and quit lying to ourselves.

Youth is blindsided by the actual situation as they first attempt to make love and, from then on, it goes downhill with a will as we get in sync with the awful lies. It usually takes one or two marriages to figure out that sex is not ever going to be as expected. Then, we accept the misery for a lifetime.

Man or woman, it ends up being unfulfilling because it is incomplete. Being sanctimonious about the suffering doesn't make it right. We spend our lives refuting the situation, acting like there is no problem. The lies convulse and confuse our humanity. It is a problem that must be admitted and dealt with. We have to admit that humans expect more. We can be so much more than a witless animal, if we just quit lying to ourselves.

As it is, coitus is a disappointing experience. No one is ready for that when it first happens because no one has admitted it.

We put unnecessary burdens on coitus but, still, you can be thankful. Nature provided. Nature did not hang sentient races out to dry or require them to just learn to cope with the failure that all previous animals endure. Any sentient race that can see that coitus is too limited an expression of love can do something about it. We blinded ourselves with lies.

The last three thousand years were unfortunate but inevitable.

Between the Flower Power movement and the LGBTQ movement, they blew the doors off of our non-sentient delusions, and opened the way for love and our sentient awareness.

Do you now see what we have been hiding from? How it has twisted our minds every which way? Can you yet admit what we have been avoiding for so long?   Can you see how it has disrupted every aspect of our existence?

Love has been compromised since the beginning. Love is not part of a limited animal's existence.   It is only for humanity. There's a catch. Love is more than just words.

Unlike the noble characteristics, love has remained a vague concept that few, if any, have ever experienced to its fullest delight.   Unlike the other characteristics, everyone seeks love with a will throughout their lifetime but never seem to attain anything more than a passing fancy or a lifetime of drudgery as its substitute.   Whereas, the noble characteristics wear away because of our deranged views that have little to do with reality.

That is the flaw in our sentience. It has all been a coverup.

Men put on their act of superiority because they have never been able to love. They have always felt exposed. They feel compromised every time they take a woman to bed and fail to provide for mutual fulfillment. Most accept that they are only an animal. More so every day.

They can seldom achieve mutual orgasm during the most important, elegant, graceful act of coitus. Men are conditioned blind to the dilemma, thereby compounding the issue.

Let me be crystal clear. There is no reason for men's failure except for the same reason that we never acknowledged the problem in the first place. We hid our heads in the sand. We never really looked. Like an idiot, our ancestors were ashamed. We buried the issue, along with our sentience, long ago.

Coitus was too critical to our ongoing existence. Without resolution (which was beyond our earliest ancestors powers), a bizarre shadow world of our sentience was created. We heaped piles of nonsense on top ever since because the failure *will not remain hidden*. The truth shall out. It has taken us three thousand years to realize this essential truth.

Sentience cannot help but recognize that the animal form of coitus is not suitable for a human. We can provide substitutes and that's fine. Rutting is not loving. We are so far gone that we don't even acknowledge the problem for what it is. The piles are so deep we don't even know what reality is.

We have been avoiding that which makes us human. Loving sex is essential to a sentient existence. Loving coitus is a bonus beyond measure that we can achieve, without pills, acrobatics, or appliances. Unassisted loving coitus is the goal.

Because loving coitus seemed impossible to attain, we lied to ourselves. Behind closed doors, alternatives were accepted. Never publicly. Because we were hiding from the truth.

Publicly, we told ourselves that a loving, mutually orgasmic, physical experience was not necessary. We try to convince ourselves that sex was just for making babies. Right. Like anyone ever really believed that. As life progresses, the truth becomes clearer and clearer. We remain an animal. All because we were scared to look under the bed.

Can you even begin to see the implications of this? The worst result of this sham is that we have never ever experienced our sentient state. We still bash through life like an animal.

Women were forced to experience, second-hand, the mind-blowing state of their mate while seldom, if ever, participating in the mind-blowing state. The man was forced to watch his mate fail to achieve the mind-blowing state while he did.

Neither likes the situation as it is. It is selfishness in a bottle for the man, if he does not find some way to fulfill his mate. It is a life of disappointment for the woman.

We have never opened our eyes and accepted the dilemma for what it is: A sentient conundrum that a sentient race must answer openly. I have answered it in every way. You're welcome.

Unaware that the loving form of unassisted coitus can exist, we have beaten around the bush, hemmed and hawed, lied through our teeth, and promoted nonsense. The irony is that our ability to love, to make humanity's existence into a loving experience, has been waiting for us all along. Not utopia. Love on a human-wide scale does not turn us into an animated movie with nothing but happy endings. It just makes us human. It puts our sentience on an even keel. We become human and love gets an even chance.

It is crucial that we blow the doors open on acknowledging and providing for the physical aspect of love. Buried with all of the other nonsense is the realization that loving coitus is possible.

Toxic masculinity, that repels so many women today, is due to this tale told by an idiot, full of sound and fury, signifying nothing. The lack of admission of the failure of coitus to provide for mutual orgasm is the tale told by an idiot. The sound and fury of men deluding themselves will dissipate like fog as men learn to love. As men learn to give ... in bed.

It is another odd irony of the bizarre existence of the prehuman that the woman becomes disgusted with the toxic masculinity of a man that she thought she knew. The repelling quality of toxic masculinity becomes the deciding factor long before she tires of unfulfilling sex. Even so, she would *still* tire of unfulfilling sex later, so no real change in the outcome. Either way, with the lies remaining, we remain a caricature of human.

Toxic masculine behaviour, as well as misogyny and most of the awful characteristics of our prehuman existence are all due to men never having learned to love. Men must learn to give and it all starts in bed. If he cannot give in bed, it creates a selfish persona and invokes misogyny. Love, the basis for a successful humanity, is based on the ability to give. It all starts in bed.

Fortunately, loving coitus is possible. Anything less would be much more difficult to convince humanity to accept with open arms. It would still be critical in the absence of loving coitus but far less likely to succeed.

Love reaches its ultimate conclusion by giving in bed. The male _gender_ *must* fulfills its ability to love. The male must finally become human, rather than a rutting animal hiding from its humanity and destroying all in its path.

This is the sentient perspective peering through all of the deceits, delusions, and confusion of the animal. It clears away the preposterous notion that "perceptions are reality" and exposes it for what it is. Prettied up, awful, pompous, stupoured, embarrassingly inept, incompetent, witless, disastrous Lying.

Quandary

As I reflect back on my own increasing understanding of our missing humanity and the mixed up state in which we remain, it becomes clearer that we have been profoundly misdirected.

We began with the situation that coitus was required for procreation and it was *not* as an intelligent being would expect.

Not only did we accept the situation as is but codified it into a belief that anything else would be 'unnatural'.

There is not a shred of sense in that concept. It is unnatural for a sentient race to run from its destiny, which is love. The only way that love ever becomes real, the only way we ever become human and gain our sanity as a sentient race, is to learn that love in a physical manner is crucial.

We went to great lengths to assure that nonsense was accepted. We compounded the nonsense as our awareness continued to question the awful situation. Can you see the pebble that started the avalanche that circumnavigate every aspect of our existence?

We feel as if we would be upsetting the balance by uttering a word. Look around. We could not upset the balance any more than we already have. We have been going against the grain of our sentient nature since the beginning. Some even blame sentience rather than the stupour of the animal. They view sentience as a mistake. The mistake was not trusting Nature. The mistake was accepting ass-covering pompous claims as directly from some nebulous god rather than a fool.

We have been avoiding that which makes us human. We still do not accept that men are lousy at coitus. All because some post-animals/pre-humans long, long ago gained the intelligence to see that there is more to love than rutting but could not admit it. In desperation, they bamboozled humanity.

More appalling, *because* they could never open up enough and, instead, buried themselves and the rest of humanity in hornswoggle and gibberish, they never realized *there is no clock for a thinking human being*.

Some purport that coitus should only be performed for the same reason as an animal. It makes babies. That is the simpleton protestations of a witless animal.

Conception of babies is crucially important, of course, but it is not all there is for a human, sentient race. One way or another, the truth shall out. In this case, the disgust with the situation, without revelation of the lies, is already beginning to have its direct affect. Coitus is becoming increasingly unpopular and 'making babies' is beginning to move towards the cliff. This is because the lies will continue to erode the situation, behind the scenes, until we admit the truth. The truth shall out, one way or another. Look around at the results of following the witless animal. We have no balance because we have refused to become human. All sound and fury.

Threshold and Transformation

It is instructive to realize that we have known of the noble characteristics that our transformed humanity should expect for thousands of years. It's paramount that we understand why we've never been able to attain them in full measure.

It has been right there in front of us for millennia. We labeled and defined the human characteristics long, long ago. Yet, somehow, we could never adopt them. We are not yet human.

Such traits as honour, integrity, dignity, empathy, compassion, etc are well understood. It's just that the prehuman animal cannot achieve them. It is based on self-respect *and* emotional stability to balance our intellect. It is education of the heart.

All of the loving, noble characteristics that we hold in such high regard are meaningless to the disturbed animal we remain. Worse yet, they seem further and further from our grasp with each passing moment. The animal is winning, especially now that the excuse of making babies has become almost secondary - a dangerous fence to stride for a stupoured, demented animal.

All we have ever really done was teach the animal to put on airs *as if* it were human. We taught the animal to *act* like a human. That was never enough. We need to *be* human.

There is a single missing trait in mankind that made the struggle to acquire the rest of the respectable human traits hopeless. This particular trait was dashed on the rocks of our inability to learn to love. We must learn to love in the fullest, most complete form that our sentient nature made clear.

We have known all along that we have failed. Men's confidence has remained dismantled. The sentient male's self-respect remained unattainable. Pompousness and toxic masculinity have been the substitute. Destruction of the male's self-image created an imbalance between male and female.

The noble characteristics have to come from within. They cannot be taught. If they are taught, they become an *act*, a facade that never reaches the soul, the heart. All of the noble characteristics are dependent on self-respect. That is the crucial missing trait that can only come from within. If one cannot believe in oneself, one cannot internalize the traits of humanity.

Most men's self-respect begins to deteriorate as they pass puberty and learn of their failure. It slowly crumbles to dust as the long years of failure to achieve love exacerbate the situation.

Once we learn to love, self-respect becomes second nature, and the human traits will follow with ease. We will *be* human, not just act out the part on the stage of the Theater of the Absurd.

Details

I have made two separate attempts to explain the details of how a man can last as long as she desires. I am uncertain how to combine the two attempts. So, I will leave both.

It is so simple that words are hardly needed, once we get over the hurdle of the nonsense we have adopted for three millennia. In the meantime, I think it may take everything a man has *to get over the hurdle of lies*. The more confident he can become that he can last indefinitely, the better his chances of staying the course and achieving success. This is only important in the short term, while the first few men are learning that all of the nonsense they have accepted for millennia is just that. Nonsense.

The Leap Never Taken

If any man had ever taken the time to think instead of scurrying into the darkest corner to hide from his shame, he would have realized it is not *his* shame. It is the shame of long-dead ancestors that were too witless, too close to the animal, to ever understand the nuances of human anatomy and animal instincts that can easily be overridden by a thinking human.

Everyone is convinced that the man is on some kind of a countdown clock. Sure, the clock starts ticking for an animal or a human male *that doesn't think things through*. The goal is to never start the clock until you are ready. There is only one event that starts the clock. Squeezing the sex glands in the crotch.

Arousal, penetration, and coitus do not equate with initiation of ejaculation. The instincts of an animal initiate ejaculation.

Every man worth his salt has the evidence that the clock can go into suspended animation. Any man worth his salt has, errrr, taken care of things for himself on occasion (rather than having it happen at an embarrassing, and inopportune moment).

Did you ever notice how difficult it is to even get the clock started in that case? There are reasons for that and it hints at why the clock should be completely under the man's control.

Some may say, "but that's not the same!" *Exactly.*

One difference is that one cannot tickle themselves. That is, essentially, what happens during 'rehearsals'. That is what makes skin on skin such a glorious event, unmatched by anything else in life. The erogenous zones, essentially, have elements similar to the two well-defined ticklish responses in other areas of the body. In this case, the muscles triggered are those in the crotch.

There are other differences, as well. They all add up to a man being able to make love the way he has always dreamed *if he takes the time and effort to think things through.*

Another difference from rehearsals is that when engaging with a woman there is movement which is often otherwise absent. That movement, when studied, makes it clear what is happening, why the animal has *no* control *and* why the human should.

An animal operates by instincts. Let me interpret "instincts". Instinct is action without thought. It is doing something the way it has always been done *because you are not thinking it through.*

Sound familiar? It should. It is the overall way in which we have operated for millennia. Like a witless animal. I am not just talking about coitus. I am talking about our whole perspective on life, although it is all due to our witless attitude towards sex.

One unfortunate instance that the animal encounters should be glaringly obvious but, somehow, it seldom really hits home. There is a driving urge for a man to dive as deep as he can. It is often even encouraged by the woman. It is a really good feeling.

Unfortunately, it triggers the *approach of climax*. It triggers the clock, the beginning of the process of ejaculation. Save it for the grand finale. It will be the finale, whether it is grand or not.

The musculoskeletal structure itself is set up to begin the discharge process by squeezing the glands when you dive deep.

In essence, it is all about the glands in the crotch that contain the vast majority of the fluids that make up the discharge of semen. When those glands are squeezed, Bang! You're done. The clock has started.

Even without the deep dive, there is one more instinct that must be avoided. This one is a little more subtle. This has to do with the movement that happens during coitus but seldom during rehearsal.

The muscles in the crotch can squeeze the glands during the normal movements of coitus, *if you are not thinking*. The pelvic muscles do not need to flex and relax during sex movements of the body. This will take a little more effort and thought than "don't do that". You will actually have to think it through.

There are two ways this 'pumping action' can happen. Both are nothing more than instincts of the animals that came before us that can be overcome easily - *if you can think like a human*. Animals perform those actions because they *can't* think. We perform them because we have not thought.

The two actions? Don't twerk and don't jerk.

Twerking is the deep dive. Find your threshold. Find out how deep you can go without triggering the clock. No more than two inches is required to stimulate the woman. You should be able to go to, at least, a 'neutral' position (similar to you normal stance), once you become confident in your ability.

Secondly, don't twerk. Don't flex the muscles in the crotch (inadvertent 'jerking'). The muscles in the crotch *are not necessary for movement and they need not flex due to erogenous (ticklish) sensation.*

The pelvic muscles are only flexed during movement because we never think about it. With forethought and practice, a man can easily avoid using them during coitus. The muscles in the legs, back, torso, etc are the only muscles necessary to provide all of the movement during coitus. There is absolutely no need to use the pelvic muscles.

It takes practice, but the crotch muscles are unnecessary for movement. You don't flex them because they are needed for movement. You flex them because no one ever really thought about it.

In the same vein is the 'ticklish' (erogenous, if you prefer) response. The muscles in the crotch get very little exercise. While performing the particular movements of coitus, it is dangerously easy for those muscles to inadvertently and unnecessarily spasm in response to the mind-bending erotic, 'ticklish' sensation. If you exercise those muscles, the ticklish response is easily overcome.

The erogenous skin on skin action is similar to tickling a person's feet with a feather or the more intense tickling of the rib cage under the arms. It is a challenge to avoid flexing the pelvic muscles due to this, but not impossible. It is also the least important matter, since the most intense sensation is only during penetration. It is all easily mastered - for a human.

It takes a *little* forethought and a *little* regular exercise of those muscles in one's crotch to be able to prevent the unwilling muscle contractions. That's it. The exercise makes the muscles more supple, more responsive to your desires which, in this case, is don't flex them. It is not a matter of relaxing them completely. Just don't contract the muscles.

If you are not enraged by the fact that this has been there all along and, somehow, your ancestors never got a clue and, further, made it nearly impossible to contemplate with an open mind, don't feel alone.

As one learns what they are doing, unless the woman is doing her best to catch you off guard (which may become a great game to see who can outlast whom), it becomes easy to last as long as one desires. Can you imagine coitus as a loving, fun event?

There is, of course, a lot of fine print, though it is no big deal. Only one more regarding early discharge. If the glands are overfull, nothing it going to stop them from being squeezed and, thus, beginning discharge. No different than the bladder being in the same condition. The answer is simple.

The other fine print is the woman's anatomy and arousal. If you want to be her lover, if you want to make love to her, for the first time in your life; essentially, the first time in the long and painful history of humanity; if you want her to climax, you will also need to know about her anatomy and what arouses her.

One of the big surprises for the unaware is that the most erotic zone of a woman (the clitoris nub or button) is *outside* of her love chamber. It is just above the vagina, usually less than a half-inch. If you aren't paying attention, you may very well miss stimulating it at all. The rest? *Within an inch or so*, just inside the opening.

Why, then, is the deep dive so enticing for both the man and the woman? Ummm, orgasm is an incredible feeling? *As is mutual orgasm* (not necessarily simultaneous, though that might make a nice goal). Stay well away from the deep dive until the grand finale.

The other aspect that I will stress, I am certain will need no emphasis once we become human. A man is easily aroused. A woman, at least in our prehuman sexual conundrum, not so much. Your efforts to arouse her need to be in everything you do. The way you touch her, the way you look at her. The way you communicate with her. In essence, the way you romance her. Romance is far more than the effort taken to get her in bed the first time. It is the effort that should last a lifetime of love. Once men gain their confidence, this will all become natural.

Oh, goodness, you will be able to spend a lifetime gazing into her eyes as she transcends this existence right along with you. I am so jealous! ... In a good way. ;~j

I have been saying for awhile now that all of the romance and loving stuff will come to a man easily once he conquers his failure. This seems so obvious to me but let me give an example of the change. Communications.

A man is so closed up today because he is a failure. Essentially, all men are a failure. It is rare indeed for a man to last as long as the woman desires. It is close to non-existent.

Can you see how the man will open up once this is no longer the case? How the male gender will be able to become loving once it no longer feels ashamed of itself? Do you see how big an impact this will have on men *and* our very existence? The unacknowledged (and unnecessary) shame has been a disaster.

I am *not* saying it will be an easy transition. It will require some men to be bold enough to think and brave enough to act to prove the case conclusively.

Just accepting the truth regarding all of our delusions and deceits would be a good start.

Above was the latest attempt to explain. The following is the older version, raging, to some extent, at the stupourdity of the ages along with a bit more analytical approach. Please do not skip it. There are a few important point, such as the exercise. There will some some repetition.

Leading into Details

The saying goes that men want sex and women want love. That portrays the dilemma poorly. Men *settle* for sex because they have not been able to fulfill the loving act as they should. Thus, they mostly remain brute animals. It is time for that to change. It's time for men to become human.

You'd better believe that every man wants to love. It's just that the animal in him lashes out when he finds he cannot, making him more animal than human. The most intimate act that should release our humanity becomes selfish.

The toxic characteristics of men grew from the compensation for the failure that has been developing for three millennia right alongside the inadvertent, unintentional selfishness of achieving orgasm without providing it. The acceptance of the impending doom of the clock has destroyed every man's chance at the truth and becoming human and loving.

Any man can last as long as *she* desires. It is easy to do. It just requires dismissing a few misconceptions and discovering what really causes unnecessary problems with *controlling* ejaculation.

All of the books that I have written over the last twelve years are about the fact that the human race has been an abysmal failure because men never learned how to love. Let me be clear. The male *gender, not just a few individuals*, needs to learn that they can love and become human. Until then...

Have you had "that talk" with your father yet? How did it go? Did he fumble around and say nothing of import? It is because he never learned how to love. Or, was he just relieved when you told him you know all about it? Let's be clear: you don't. There are very few men that have overcome the animal's limitations. Most only know what the animal passed on: Rut. Stick it in and get it over with or hang on for dear life. The latter is the animal's interpretation of what it means to be human. It is demented.

The easy part is understanding how to love a woman physically in the most elegant manner of coitus. The difficult part is overcoming the implications, obfuscation, and refutation of what is missing. The nonsense we have endured for oh, so very long, makes it seem complicated.

Before too many generations have passed, loving coitus will become second nature. It will become as easy as learning to ride a bike and much more satisfying for all. Men will finally be in control of that which makes them human.

We made a few bad assumptions way back when. The first bad assumption is that a man's ejaculation is on a countdown timer from the time he begins making love. That is the most wrong-headed assumption we ever made. It is completely wrong.

It is on a clock for an animal that can't think things through. _We think_. Well, we _can_ think. We can change what we do so that the clock never starts until we want it to do so.

Secondly, well, hell, the previous paragraph leads to everything else. The feeling men have that it is hopeless and helpless follows from that. The feeling that they can have no control over the act of making love comes from that. The toxic behavior. The nerdy behaviour. Those that give up on life. All revolves around the lie we have always told ourselves.

The feeling that he is fated to be forever lousy at coitus and, thus, all of his miserable life stems from that. A man's inability to fulfill his humanity comes from that.

All of it begins because we never made a simple distinction. The timer starts _when the ejaculation process begins_. The key is, of course, not starting the ejaculation process.

All of the conflict, confusion, contention, misogyny, and inequitable treatment of women is due to men being confounded by a single problem. Now, men can love and become human.

Men have been takers and women givers. It all starts in bed. It doesn't need to remain that way. It is an animal's environment.

It is only the instincts of an animal that have held us back. We have believed there is nothing to be done. We throw up our hands and say, "We're only human!"

Are you kidding me???!!! We should have always been saying, "Omigosh, we are human!"

All because humanity's intellect grew in the backdrop of an animal's instincts and we never realized it. Our sentient awareness remains hostage to our inability to love fully; without impediment. How hampered our sentience is seems clear when considering that it took three millennia to realize that loving coitus is missing and all it takes to overcome the failure just comes down to overcoming an animal's rutting instincts. We accepted the sexual instincts of an animal without a second thought for the last three thousand years!

It is nothing more than instincts that a human can easily override. That is seriously embarrassing for all present and past generations. If you feel dumbfounded, don't feel alone.

There is probably no end to the learning, once we get it through our heads that men can learn to love. Humanity will open up like a blossoming flower. Humanity can finally celebrate its sentient existence. What is described below is enough for any man to last as long as *she* desires.

Passing some mysterious threshold of two or three minutes means nothing. It is only meaningful to love your lover the way *she* desires, to the same level of enjoyment that the man always experiences. Thus, the act of coitus becomes human.

Details

Loving coitus (i.e. mutual orgasm) is just a matter of the man understanding what causes the discharge to *begin* and, then, recognizing and overcoming instincts *that cause the process to begin for an animal*.

The point is to avoid ever letting the ejaculation process begin rather than holding on for dear life after ejaculation has already begun. Once it begins, it is all but over. *That* is when the clock starts. Don't let it begin until you are ready. If you read any of the drivel on the web, it invariably discusses how to *delay discharge*. There is never any mention of delaying the beginning of the process. That is always taken as fait accompli. Worse yet, delaying discharge is damaging to the physiology (I get into that in previous books). Just don't start until the time is right.

Men have always accepted that starting the process of ejaculation was unavoidable. ***Big mistake.***

The big picture is that the sex glands in the crotch, when squeezed, begin ejaculation. Nothing else. That's it. It is only instincts that cause the sex glands to be squeezed. An animal can do nothing about it.

There are a few things to learn, a few instincts to overcome. They concern one issue: squeezing the sex glands in the crotch.

The erotic spasming response, similar to the ticklish response of other muscles, potentially - *not necessarily* - twinges the pelvic muscles to squeeze the sex glands in the crotch.

When uncontrolled, it can cause a twinging of the orgasmic muscles in the crotch, which squeezes the sex glands. The response of the muscles in the crotch to the sexually erotic sensation *can be controlled by any* human.

It is also the least important instinct as it only really comes into play during penetration. If you feel the crotch muscles twinge, take a moment before beginning any activity. Give the organs a moment to recover. Look up 'edging' for further information. If you have been exercising and gained enough experience, this should not be the case. The exercises described below can help you become familiar with the muscles in order to make the muscles responsive to your desires, unresponsive to the instincts of an animal.

Otherwise, that ticklish sensation is the amazing background sensitivity that plays such a huge a part in making coitus such a mind-blowing experience. That is a good thing when controlled.

There are two other instinctual reactions that cause the squeezing of the sex glands in the crotch. Either can easily trigger the beginning of the ejaculation process thus, the early end to what would otherwise be a loving act.

One of those instincts is as simple to overcome as it is to understand. Men don't twerk until the lady sings. Women should.

Thrusting the pubic bone (crotch) forward to the furthest extent squeezes the glands decisively (i.e. twerking). It starts the clock. If you do that, it will be over soon. The *animal's* instinct is to immediately plunge as deeply as possible.

Women often never move at all or only slightly due to fear of causing the experience to end too soon and being blamed for the early end. The woman should twerk for all the man can bear.

In the case of twerking (undisciplined full forward thrust), the musculoskeletal structure forces the pubic bone (as well as the pelvic muscles) to squeeze the sex glands. It will invariably cause the beginnings of orgasm, and process of ejaculation in the man's case. Understand how deep is safe. Start as shallow as possible and go from there. It is a simple effort.

The second instinct is more subtle and will take some effort. It is the most elusive characteristic of the orgasmic instincts and the most difficult to tame. The technique mentioned above can help with this, also, though it is not crucial.

The pelvic muscles have *nothing to do with movement.* They have everything to do with squeezing the sex glands. The pelvic muscles do not *need* to flex until you desire orgasm. When flexed, they squeeze the sex glands which begins the dreadful countdown clock. It is the most common reason for the early end to what would otherwise be a loving experience.

All of the movements involved in coitus need to be done carefully until it becomes natural not to flex the pelvic muscles. Changing directions is one of the most important points to which to pay attention. It is very easy, but unnecessary, to flex the pelvic muscles during the transition of direction. Don't jerk when changing directions. Make it as smooth a transition as possible and *don't flex those crotch muscles.*

The muscles in the thighs, back, and torso all that are required for movement. The crotch muscles add nothing to movement. They only flex due to the witless instincts of the animal. They don't have any effect on movement. They just pump the glands.

None of the movements during sex *require* the pelvic muscles. It is just a matter of realizing this and avoiding using the pelvic muscles for the movements involved in loving coitus. This is what I term 'jerking'. It just takes practice.

Don't twerk, don't jerk.

Do you see? It is all about the muscles. It is little different from learning to ride a bike or walk.

The muscle response (jerking) or deep plunge (twerking) squeezes the glands containing the fluids that begins the cascade to orgasm. It is as simple as that. It will become a fine art.

Save the deep plunge for the finale, when *she* is ready.

Holding on for dear life is *exactly* what a man does *not* want to do as it amounts to *flexing the pelvic muscles*!

I'll reiterate: *don't squeeze the glands!*

One more critical point. If the glands are <u>already overfull</u>, squeezing the glands is unavoidable. The solution is obvious.

With uncontrolled instincts in play, it begins and ends in seconds or, at best, a very few minutes. The instincts are rarely, if ever, *consciously* considered. The squeezing of the muscles is the usual response to the beginnings of ejaculation which, as you can see, is *exactly* the wrong response.

One technique to consider is movement that does not involve movement of the crotch muscles at all. Call it whole-body-movement for lack of a better term. The less you flex the crotch, the easier it is to avoid the beginnings of ejaculation. That doesn't mean you cannot move the pelvis. It just makes it easier when it does not move at all.

The man must keep his thrusts relatively shallow until the *intentional* finale (i.e. don't twerk, don't thrust as far as possible until 'the lady sings'). Only about two inches is required to stroke the woman's every erotic nerve-ending inside and out. The shaft itself strokes the most sensitive arousal point (i.e. clitoral nub) that is just *outside* and *above* the opening (by ~ one-half inch or less). It is critical to realize its location. It is easy to miss stroking the most erotic point on the woman's body. Since it is outside of her love chamber, it is necessary to position correctly.

The other major erogenous zone for a woman is the clitoral wishbone, much less than two inches inside. The shaft stroking the two clitoral erogenous zones should be more than enough.

The woman's twerking assists her orgasm in the same way.

Think on this. Now, once you both begin to achieve orgasm, you can leave the lights on and look into each other's loving eyes as you each achieve the transcendent state of orgasm.

Just be careful and go very slow until you understand 1) how deep is safe (it should be far more than two inches as you progress) and 2) how to avoid contracting (or, worse, spasming) the muscles in the crotch.

An additional technique, if necessary, is to stop all activity at the first sign that you are becoming overstimulated until the sense of overstimulation is gone. It should not be necessary with exercise and practice but may be useful while still learning. This is called 'edging' by some.

It is a learning process. We are human. That is what we do. That is what we are *supposed* to do. In the case of coitus, we have avoided the learning process, thus remaining a dumbfounded animal, wrecking everything, for millennia.

These points are straightforward and will become natural, thus replacing the instincts of an animal. It will become natural within a generation or two of the time that humanity begins to succeed at love in its most essential physical form. Little real learning should be necessary within a generation or two. It will be absorbed from the confidence of one's elders amidst a few minor insights that may be commonly known, like, "don't twerk, don't jerk, and exercise. Become familiar with the muscles."

The exercises are just as crucial in youth as it is for later in life. They are not so much about building muscles as it is making the muscles responsive to your demands and unresponsive to animal instincts. It is only about two minutes.

There are other benefits as you age, like not wearing diapers. The immediate advantages, even in youth, include making the muscles supple and responsive and avoid any untoward tendency to spasm or contract unnecessarily.

Avoiding the deep plunge and discovering one's depth limits is just a matter of paying attention.

In case you missed it, you are human. Controlling those responses is as easy as walking on two legs. Now, you will be able to open your eyes to the one you adore while loving her.

I spend around *two* minutes (only two!) exercising those muscles daily, and, also, *not* exercising them. That is, not flexing the crotch muscles, while using the muscles in the torso, legs, etc that *are* necessary for movement only.

On the back with knees flexed and swinging towards each other and away works well for me. Flex the pelvic muscles as you swing the knees towards each other. Relax the muscles as you swing the knees apart. Thirty times, approximately thirty seconds. This will help you become familiar with muscles and also, prepare you to even control the ticklish response. Then, hold them flexed for another thirty times while swinging the knees in and out. Then, leave them relaxed for another minute will working the leg, torso, and hip muscles to get the pelvic muscles familiar with avoiding flex them due to movement. That's it!

I would expect a lot of variation on these exercises. Rote should become a thing of the past for a human race. The exercises could also be practiced during walking, sitting, or any form of exercise.

I would also suggest alternating between the exercise above and doing them with the legs stretched out fully. Obviously, you are not swinging the knees, in this case.

Another good, errr, non-exercise is standing knee bends *without* flexing the pelvic muscles. What is termed 'sexercise' would be a perfect time to practice this.

There may be others that you decide you prefer.

Twerking movement can be especially helpful in learning to control the muscles. Practice reversing direction smoothly, avoiding the deep plunge, and estimate how deep is safe.

In essence, you are trying to do two things. Condition the pelvic muscles *and* become familiar with *not* using them when unnecessary and detrimental to the act of loving coitus.

You might also want to look up 'Kegel exercises'.

There will be more to learn about avoiding flexing as you make love but this will prepare you by becoming familiar with the act of leaving those muscles relaxed while flexing the muscles that *are* necessary for movement. I'm sure more exercises will be conceived.

I really doubt this will be the last written on exercises to make it easier to avoid unwanted orgasms. I have already rewritten this a dozen times as I learned more and more. I expect there is more yet that others will discover once we remove the blinders.

Another caution. Self-stimulation (or dress rehearsals, or masturbation, if you prefer) needs to be done carefully. If you abuse your member, it will come back to haunt you. *Do not inadvertently do so!* It will make it almost impossible to avoid the beginnings of ejaculation. The triggers become deeply set.

There is no reason to abuse your member, *if you realize what triggers an orgasm.*

The development of the spasming response due to abuse of your member can be disastrous.

It can be difficult to achieve orgasm when, errr, taking the matter in hand, *because* the normal motions of coitus are *not* the norm during self-stimulation.

Also, the tickle response is absent. A person cannot tickle themselves.

The subliminal urge to rush through it can become a habit that follows through when attempting to last as long as *she* desires. Do not attain that habit. It is really hard to break.

Abuse, which can happen in attempts to achieve orgasm, or rush to completion, will make the spasm response *extremely* difficult to overcome. *Do not abuse your member.*

Humanity should learn to approach masturbation unabashedly. It is far better than letting the lack of release get under one's skin. I'm not expecting that to change in a hurry. Once we lose our sense of shame regarding sex, maybe we will have a chance.

Also, don't let your child (either sex, really) be mutilated by circumcision. In the U.S., it is considered a Christian tradition. IT IS NOT A CHRISTIAN TRADITION!!!!

There is no rational reason for the mutilation of circumcision, though there are many irrational, insane reasons.

A circumcised person can still achieve controlled ejaculation but it may be more of a challenge (I was circumcised. I suspect it made it that much more difficult to succeed at loving coitus, but it was still possible).

The biggest thing for me is that I am certain circumcision leaves a psychic shock when they slice it away, no matter the anesthetics or sharpness of the scalpel. There's just no need for it. It is sick. It is an animal reveling in causing pain.

I would say that, no matter where you are in the world, it would be worth checking before you have a baby. In many places, they will slice without asking.

The most important things to know are: don't twerk or jerk (i.e. don't dive deep or flex/spasm the pelvic muscles, respectively) until the lady sings. Become familiar with the pelvic muscles and control them. Be sure you understand her arousal, erogenous zones, and desires. Communicate. Become human.

Just remember, you are human. Of course you can control the muscles and your own discharge. Keep in mind that overfull glands means they *will* be squeezed. Do not become discouraged if it takes a while to adjust and make things work. At this point, it is all new. The older you are, the more time should be expected to adjust as there are more bad habits necessary to overcome.

You can now proceed to engage in loving coitus, mutual orgasm, enthusiastically in a human manner while gazing into your lover's eyes with the lights on. Love can finally mature into its sentient form. We can become human.

I apologize for concentrating on the men's issues but men have the most to learn, by far.

There is another point that I have not highlighted ever before. The closest I came was mentioning that, after men gain their confidence, their self-respect, the rest will come easily.

While that is true, it is not enough, at this point. During the transition into that state, there are a few things that a man will need to consider. After we are human, it will be as obvious as the Earth beneath your feet as men open up.

Not only does a woman's orgasm take some time but, at least at this point, so does arousal for many women. I think it is very possible that this, also, may change, once women become convinced that they, also, can expect to achieve orgasm during coitus on a consistent basis. Their enthusiasm may even match that of the man.

The point is that, if a man does not take his time achieving the woman's high arousal, before beginning coitus, she may never achieve orgasm. I would love to see a book by a woman on these matters. Of course, the book never made sense as long as men don't last. The orientation for a man needs to change radically. It is not all about him. It is all about loving and giving, not just pleasing oneself. Selfishness needs to be gone.

For women, just make sure you are doing the opposite of what I've recommended for men and you should orgasm easily. Flex and twerk like crazy or as much as he can bear, which should improve over time. Relish the erotic feelings that cause the spasms to engage. Encourage them. Communicate.

I am becoming more and more convinced that, as we open up and become more comfortable with the change and the insights, we will learn a lot more.

Let me give a new insight that has been rattling around in my head for awhile, just as an example of how far we have to go to really understand what is going on. Men's inability to open up. It is only a new insight in that I understand it now. I mention it in passing in earlier books, but the link between men's closed persona and their shame is becoming more and more obvious. Men are in a catch-22 situation - damned if you do, damned if you don't. To whom are they supposed to open up regarding the most crucial aspect of their existence that is not going their way? It is so bad that they cannot even open up to themselves!

It is true that, if we had begun, millennia ago, with our sentience fully in tact, the man would have been screaming for answers, thus realizing much sooner that no man knows what he is doing and, thus, succeeded sooner. But, no, we were mostly animals.

All of the loving will become natural once we remove the blinders. We will no longer be in hiding, and we can look for further ways in which to improve the loving. I don't mean just the physical aspects, either. That is only the beginning that expands to a much more loving and caring perspective on life.

I've mentioned 'communicate' a lot in this section. I've also mentioned men's future openness. The two combine to take this all to the next level.

Once our natural desire to love is established and reinforced by men gaining confidence that they can love, the rest of our loving nature will come to the fore. Communication will become the natural result. Men are all locked up inside themselves because of the failure and shame.

This goes well beyond the intimate relationship. Humanity can become a balanced, emotionally stable, rational loving race of sentient beings that share their existence.

This is why I am not really concerned about men learning the finer points of loving. Only shame and failure have stunted men.

A few further notes as I progress. First of all, after six books I am annoyed to find that the excellent term that I had created, 'indefinitely delayed ejaculation', has already been adopted to cover the case of the poor man that can't ever ejaculate.

Secondly, there is a lot better term: controlled ejaculation. I still like 'indefinitely delayed ejaculation' better but I don't wish to cause any confusion. There is enough of that already.

I haven't even touched on any of the subjects besides men lasting long enough that are crucial to making love. The rest of it will come easily, once men are certain that they don't need to fail at the most essential task: lasting long enough. In the meantime, though, as we seek our way, it is at least worth mentioning a few key points.

The emotional loving, the romance, the foreplay, the loving attitude, the gentle, equitable treatment of women, the rainbow loving of women that has been lacking all falls right out of what I have been explaining. They are results of becoming human.

Also, remember, it is the woman that gets pregnant, not you. So, if coitus is off the table, deal with it. If you care for her enough, you'll stick around. Find some other way in which to achieve mutual orgasm.

I have to highlight, though, that there are other ways to *assure* (a condom is not assurance; the pill has drawbacks. the woman being forced to futz with her hormones by taking a pill is futzing with her physiology) impregnation never takes place while engaging in coitus.

I must emphasize before I end this section that *any man* can learn to make love. It will be a challenge for the first generation. They will be scared spitless that they will fail, they will be fighting against three thousand years of conditioning that they cannot succeed and shouldn't even think about it.

As the confidence builds that any man can last as long as she desires, the floodgates will open.

Every man, sooner or later, will learn that they can love in the most natural manner possible while looking adoringly into the eyes of their lover. That is the point. We become human when the *male gender* becomes human.

For later generations, as the knowledge becomes commonly known and widely accepted, it will be much easier. It will be almost as easy as learning to walk. Further improvements should be expected as our eyes are opened.

There will always be more to learn once we remove the blinders. That's what humans do. I have provided enough to get our sentience and our full-on loving started.

The Struggle

There has always been a struggle on the two fronts on which we have attacked the perplexity of our humanity dating back at least three thousand years. The two fronts, love and sex, of course, finally converge on loving coitus.

The core of the problem becomes glaringly obvious as you consider past efforts regarding sex. Like the Kinsey, and Masters and Johnson studies, which are more recent examples of their predecessor, the *Kama Sutra*, written by Vatsyayana Mallananaga. They are demolished before they ever begin.

In each case, including Mallananaga, their work is undone by the past. They have all accepted men's surrender to the clock without a second thought. Since men don't do better at coitus, they cannot do better. All because we began, long ago, as an animal. They believe what their predecessors accepted and passed on to them: there is no loving coitus. Men cannot last. There is nothing to be done. It's all some foolish mystery. Let the misery and lies and shame continue.

Mallananaga at least attempted to provide a solution that worked but, all in all, it has never changed. It was a valiant effort but, essentially ineffectual, way too complicated, and never addressed the real issue. He accepted that men have a limitation that cannot be overcome *because his predecessors told him so*. He states very clearly what his predecessors believed: there is nothing to be done about men's limitation, so Mallananaga attempted to find a way around the problem.

The more recent efforts, of course, being distorted by the heaps of nonsense we have adopted over the intervening three millennia, surrender without a fight. "It is hopeless, so just get used to it." They completely succumb to the dumb beast.

But, that is just on the sexual front. Then, there is the loving front.   Jesus, Buddha, Emerson, James Taylor, and London Grammar are four my favorites, but there are so many, that have attempted to explore love.   Just about any lyricist or poet has explored love. In their youth, it is often happy, reveling lyrics.

That all turns to ashes as the shock of failure sets in for the male and the curious behaviour of the male, as well as disappointment set in for the woman, the distortions to reality begin to form. The songs reflect their misery and the failure of love as they age.   The bitterness creeps in.   The bitterness is creeping in earlier and earlier. We should be celebrating.

The unrealistic resolution regarding love that we have lived with for at least two thousand years is that love is based on willpower alone.   Nose-to-the-grindstone approach.   It is clear *that* has never worked. There is not much love in this prehuman world and it is abandoned at the drop of a hat. Insanity reigns.

The concept of love, without its physical expression being fulfilled, can never answer. Unless a sentient being <u>*gives*</u> love in its physical form or has a solid expectation of such, one becomes a demented animal. It is mostly about expectations, at this point.

No one can *will* themselves to love, while failing to love. I've attempted to explain the woman's position in this debacle in many of the other books.   I'll just note here that women have more characteristics of sentient maturity than the male.   That doesn't mean that they can't be dragged down by the animal. Many are. Many women have always bought into the delusions.

Ironically, the LGBTQ movement has scared heterosexuals spineless.   This also shows how deeply the paradigms of nonsense have been drilled.   First of all, heterosexuals are erroneously convinced that coitus can't compete.   They'll never state it that way but that is what it amounts to.   They are, of course, wrong.   Men can love through heterosexual loving coitus. Once they learn to do so, LGBTQ will not seem like an adversary.   Physical love, in any form, is better than none. Secondly, can loving coitus wins out for the heterosexual.

My favorite of all of the more contemporary seekers of love is Emerson.   My overall favorite seeker, though, is the unknown author of Pandora's Box. That person was truly amazing. Once all of the blind embellishments, critiques, and connotations, and purposeful delusions are discounted, Pandora's Box says it all.

Woman gave a gift to mankind. When a man opened it, chaos was released. Do you see? Do you see the source of our chaos that Pandora's Box states so clearly? The myth is far more truth than fiction. Men have always known the source of their chaos. They were just never willing to admit it to others or themselves.

Do you see the hope that was left in the box? That love can succeed? The myth is incredibly insightful. The hope that was left in the box was for men to learn that they are not controlled by an animal's instincts or a clock. The chaos can end. A man can overcome the limitations that make him no more than an animal and allow him to become a loving human. Love and sex converge. That Pandora's Box saw all of this three thousand years ago staggers the mind.

Within a few hundred years of Pandora's Box, maybe the very first example of intentional misinformation, in order to hide from the truth, was created. The Garden Of Eden. Blame it all on women, instead of facing the truth.

My story

I want to tell you a short version of my own story.

Like most sane people, I started out expecting everything to turn up roses. It took years, decades for it to finally sink in.

Training in my youth had given me no notions or options.

I was lousy at sex. The training, in essence was, just don't think about it. You are a man, whatever that was supposed to mean. Sex was just something you do. Stick it in and get it over.

So, why was it I felt so bad after every instance of 'making love' that was no more than rutting? That had me baffled for decades until about a dozen years ago when I realized, no, there was supposed to be something special about sex. I put my foot down and began to explore in earnest.

It's funny, as I look back on it. I had been looking for what is wrong with humanity all my life, while it was right there in front of me. I had put together so many pieces of the puzzle before the final realization.

The gentler nature of women. The obnoxious qualities pertaining to men. The utter insanity that everyone tries to pin on individuals, never admitting that it is a race-wide phenomenon that just makes its appearance differently across the spectrum of humanity for various reasons. All of the commotion of humanity had become clear, except for why.

I had already begun to realize that there were a lot of men that were lousy at coitus. I had also been investigating the nonsense on the web and elsewhere regarding making coitus last. I had also studied religions, institutions, and cultures. Outside forces.

So, when I was finally honest with myself regarding how lousy I was at coitus, it was the final link in the chain. It all fell in place like an avalanche. It wasn't such a leap as it will be for most of you. We can be human. We've always known it.

I hope I have paved the way to make your acceptance of our humanity a lot smoother than mine.

Back to reality

If you inspect the Flower Power generation closely, it tells so much more. The only people that could have *ever* linked the two concepts of love and sex irreversibly is a youthful generation. The only person to blow the doors wide open, at this late date, had to have lived a full life and never accepted the misery as status quo.

Only in our youth do we retain the innocence to question openly all of the awful lies that each previous generation finally accepts as the stupour of delusions and misinformation closes in.

It took an old male to put all of the pieces together in a coherent manner. If it wasn't for the youths breakthroughs, I would never have been able to take it further.

The shock of attaining puberty and *not* being able to love a woman is a disaster that is repeated endlessly, wearing away at the individual's perspective and self-image over a lifetime. As our sentience begins to take center stage, it becomes clearer. It is just weird how youth rebels against something they can't even pin down. It is downright fascinating, in fact.

As failure to realize that men are not on a clock continues, another generation gives up hope, states that 'we are only human', and moves on to convince the next generation that it is hopeless. Those that have spent a lifetime being deceived guard their backs with a vengeance. They cannot admit the truth. They would rather turn the world upside down.

All humans are born with love in their bones. It is obvious when you consider it. There are two crucial parts of sentience: love and honesty. Without those two, we are not human.

Only one hundred years ago, the conversation that the Flower Power generation began in earnest was all but completely unknown. A woman having an orgasm? Unheard of! Certainly never mentioned or considered.

Ever since the Flower Power generation inadvertently began to expose the truth, it has just become an increasing mishmash of confusion. As we made our first serious attempt to claim our sentient prize of love against all of the deception, delusion, and confusion, we floundered, once again, because we could not attain the goal of loving coitus any better than in the past.

Even without the success of unassisted loving coitus we would need to face the truth of the situation and figure out an *honest* way forward. Any way you look at it, we have to admit the lies and deal with them. Our most ancient institutions are full of lies. It just seemed tidier to make loving coitus available in its most beautiful, natural, elegant form.

You're welcome. Nature didn't let us down.

The towering, cowering fear of the male makes it clear that men remain in a gibbering stupour. It is clear that they can't really think at all while in such a state.

Don't blame men for our predicament. Blame the inexorable, merciless inertia of history and emergence of sentience from an animal that initially didn't know anything and coped with the failure in the most awful manner possible.

The disconcerting *subconscious* feeling of failure leaves men undone, floundering, bewildered, devastated. They have been forced to put on an act for three thousand years to cover their failure because they were blinded to the problem since birth.

Men will continue to live an awful, unfulfilling life and lie and continue to wreak havoc on our existence until they learn how to love - physically. The lack would derange anyone. There is no reason for it other than inertia and the stupour of the ages.

Love, along with honesty, are necessary to free our sentient awareness. They *are* the basis for a sentient reality. Without the physical expression of love, our sentient awareness remains trapped in the subconscious as we lie to ourselves and distort our sentient reality. Sentience is all about love and an honest assessment of reality. Nature changed the game. For the better.

It is not a terminal condition. We can be human.

All of the chaos we have endured is due to the lack of one simple insight. Men can love in the most important way that really counts. It releases our sentience from the animal.

All the little pieces

All of the little pieces fit snugly into the puzzle that represents, on the grandest scale, a sentient reality.

Loving coitus is only a crucial, yet small, piece of the mosaic of a sentient reality and the final emergence and flourishing of our sentient awareness that has been blunted since we first emerged as a race attempting to be more than an animal.

We created whole institutions intent on carrying on the lie.

The quandary of the animal's rutting coitus versus human loving coitus left us undone. We had to have coitus to provide babies. Only rutting was available. We could not grasp that human, loving coitus was just as easily available (except, maybe, the author of Pandora's Box). It took three thousand years to upend the misdirection and chaos and realize the hope.

The awful saying 'perception is reality' explains just how detached we have become from the truth and our sentience. Most of the world believes that whatever lie you concoct, can be your reality. Sorry to break it to you, but, no, reality is tangible. Prehumans are the only ones around that can't see that. We are all such a bundle of demented lies and stupour.

We revert to the animal at the drop of a hat. The least little disturbance and we revert to our vicious animal ways and say, "we're only human". We have yet to become human.

The man wants authority because he has nothing else. It is a substitute for the control that he lacks. It is awful and it is playing out in the worst way possible today. He has used that false authority to distort the panorama of sentience.

Once we become an emotionally stable, rational, balanced, fulfilled, sentient race, we will no longer be accepting lies to fill the gap. We will no longer be filled with an unconscious dread that leads to paranoia, violence, and lies. All because of a failure that we can't admit. We will no longer go to war because of prickly, paranoid, male pride that is nothing more than a coverup, a distraction, a temper tantrum to hide from the truth, once we learn to love and live as a sentient human has every right.

Contending with the inconsistencies of our existence breaks us down as we proceed through life. We become overwhelmed by the distorted reality as our sentient awareness goes unheeded.

The distortions and deceits initiated by the lack of loving coitus, the cover up if you will, has continued for three thousand years, infecting every aspect of our human life and awareness. In all ways, we have adopted an animal's viewpoint rather than a human, sentient perspective. The 'perceived' reality that we have adopted is the reality of a mad animal.

Transition

One of the most difficult fragments to describe of this tremendously complex tapestry is the effect of past generations. We've been stuck in a rut (unintentional pun) for three millennia through inertia alone. Each generation is conditioned by the *previous generation* to conceive of itself as animal. As questions occur, the older generation knocks them down with stupidity, with rationalizations, with lies.

We have convinced ourselves that the sentient state is composed of liars rather than the obvious result of the demented state of an animal attempting to become sentient.

We have not been able to get out of our own way.

Each new generation has been set up to fail by the mounds of preconceptions absorbed during our earliest years. Each generation slowly chips away at the falsehoods.

Each has always been well indoctrinated and thoroughly hobbled to failure by *their* immediate predecessors. They pass on corrupted knowledge and a bizarre outlook, setting the stage for acceptance of the failure as the next generation achieves puberty and finds coitus wanting. Hidden deep beneath all of the flotsam is the fact that coitus doesn't work as a sentient race of beings expects. Everyone becomes convinced over a lifetime, "that's the way it is." "We're only human." They have no idea.

In maybe the weirdest twist of all, each generation is set up to accept failure and, yet, *they never see it coming.* It is so incongruous that we celebrate coitus and, yet, never mention that it doesn't work as advertised. The disappointment runs deep.

Men and women are both surprised by the failure of loving coitus. Both often make the same mistake of believing it is just them (the men) or just their lousy luck (the women). No one ever seems to suspect it is a common trait for men.

Does this begin to penetrate your brain? How could an individual possibly delude themselves so thoroughly and confusingly? There has been a massive (inadvertent) campaign to hide from the truth that men are lousy at coitus. The prehuman stupour at its finest.

Both men and women usually believe it is just their individual problem. Other men can do much better. The saddest, for me, is when the woman blames herself. That is just sick.

Let's be clear, in two ways. *No one*, not the man or the woman, likes it when coitus doesn't achieve orgasm for both. The problem is compounded because men have little choice. They (essentially) must have sexual release. Deep in their subconscious lurks the realization that the woman is not enjoying the act nearly as much as they are. The combination undermines.

It thereby becomes a selfish act for the man and a selfless act for the woman. Neither suffices. It needs to be and can only become a loving act when it is a loving act for both.

Depending on which survey or research you refer to, it is somewhere well north of 70% of men *can't last long enough to bring a woman to orgasm during unassisted coitus.* For many reasons, my own estimation is much closer to 100%. Like everything else, the lies distort the situation, especially when it comes to coitus. It seems certain that some men last as long as she desires. From what I can tell, it is very, very, very few.

What makes it even more ludicrous is that, because most men can only last two or three minutes, that was defined as success. It is a blatant, sad attempt to cover up what is obvious. Men are lousy at sex, until they become human. Do you see the scared little boy? The man that releases holy hell to distract from it?

Do you see how insidious and disastrous the actual situation is? The man believes *his* failure is unusual. Proclaiming two minutes as success doesn't help at all. Especially since he was never told to expect failure. He has been picked out to be lousy at coitus. There's no way for him to verify that it is not just him. Who is he going to ask? The paranoia created cannot be overstated. It is consistent with the awful behaviour of men. We see it all around us. Any facade of humanity is overrun.

The more we erroneously understand, the more miserable we become. Until we learn to love.

Many women, after encountering man after man that is lousy at coitus only believe that they have been terribly unlucky or, the most awful conclusion, that there is something wrong with them. How incredible that statement is cannot be overstated. It is another example of how well conditioned humanity is.

What is worse for all is the rift that has causes between the genders. Staggeringly, what brings it all to a head is not the lousy sex but the awful behaviour of men. This is what repulses women. The insidious effect of failure on men's behaviour *and hiding from it* has been our undoing.

All of this tells you just how deep the prehuman conditioning goes to hold us back from reality. Three thousand years.

Can you see what a monstrous mentality this creates as individuals see themselves as picked out for awful results regarding the most loving act of existence, never realizing it is the whole damn prehuman race? Can you begin to see the awful mentality as the human race continues to delude itself?

We repeatedly, with every new generation, convince ourselves that the failure of loving coitus is unavoidable. We convince ourselves, "that's just the way it is" and "we are only human". Then, we turn around and act like there's no problem with coitus.

The devastation creeps up on a man because of the preconditioning to completely ignore the problem. After all, they are masters of the universe! - but, paltry failed creatures where it really counts. They need to become masters of themselves.

Do you see the toxic masculinity glaring through? Do you see the compensation for failure that cannot be remedied in any way, except one. Do you see the selfish effect? Do you see the sad, mad little boy attempting to *act* like a man. The answer has always been there but men were too undone, too bewildered to take a close enough look to realize it. The game was rigged from the start. The confusion is legend. The results disastrous.

The devastation of love bewilders the woman. She has been waiting all these millennia for it to change and release her.

All of the religious profundities only apply to the prehuman.

Let me make it clear, again. It is not hopeless for a human race that can get out of its own way. It would be a huge leap forward to openly admit the problem. I just could not stop there. That is not the final answer. Nature is better than that. It will take skillful use of our intellect and awareness to overcome the instincts of an animal but it is far from impossible.

Instead, like an animal we attacked our sentience. Many convinced themselves that sentience, knowledge (i.e. Garden of Eden, original sin) was the problem, never realizing that it was the lack of knowledge, the lies, that have done us in. As if sentience, rather than our witless past, were the problem.

As if Nature had not done its job. Nature provided all of the tools required for humanity to become a fulfilled sentient race. It has been up to humanity to use its wits to overcome the time limit that only an animal's instincts make real.

Take a look at all of the studies regarding coitus. The supported conclusion is that it is all a mystery.

Two minutes is success, hooray! I don't know a man alive that is satisfied with two minutes.

A *man* can control the clock completely. He is human.

Men have had so much - let me think of a good technical word - crap beaten into their brains by their ancestors that they don't even bother to look up and realize that those ancestors were dumber than empty intergalactic space.

I think of women as these entities that are full of love. You can't tell me I'm wrong. I see it every day. They are, for the most part, mature, loving, emotionally stable individuals. While it is often in hiding, for good reason, it is there. Unless it is beaten out of them.

Nowadays, it is often beaten out of them. Worse yet, many are beginning to accept the male role model as they also become brainwashed that we are nothing better than an animal. If you look closely at these women, they are either fully controlled by a male or have found their way through life by mimicking or manipulating the male. The female caricatures of toxic masculinity are awful to contemplate.

It is truly horrifying to think that we have thrown up our hands for three thousand years, accepting all of this pain for the most simple, *mindless* reason that has no reason to exist.

Men take and women give and it all starts in bed. It doesn't need to be that way.

It has been a comedy of errors for three thousand years. It has been inertia of miscommunications, misunderstanding and confusion of the animal that never attained its sentient state. It has been accepting the (demented) animal state as human.

The male has *believed* that he cannot love. All because no one is willing to admit what is missing.

Instead, we create a paltry definition of love that any demented animal could meet. It is an awful caricature of love.

The male's broken genetics (the nefarious Y chromosome) or some such nonsense is blamed. That is how desperate we are to hide from the truth.

The truth is there before us every single day and, yet, we avoid facing it. Man considers himself doomed to remain nothing more than a brute animal that is trained to play the part of a human by his more sentient, emotionally balanced female counterpart that *always* gives in bed.

The disaster that we accepted was that the man and the woman were cast in their parts by nature, genetics, or some mysterious force. Let me explain 'mysterious' for you. It is a mystery to a dumbfounded animal that never attained its sentience.

I will reiterate and expound. *Nature provided.*

Nature provided the most magnificent scheme to transform the dumb animal into something incredible: a loving, emotionally stable, balanced race of sentient beings that are equally and equitably treated. Not just the woman's treatment but the treatment of all of the human race that the prehuman treats so awfully. The human race can create an existence worthy of its sentience. All we ever had to do was get out of our own way, accept our sentient circumstances and be open to embrace what Nature provided.

Nature provided the means by which we can overcome sentient coital failure. The wits and honesty to study the anatomy and see past the instincts and witless animal's take on sex, as well as life and existence.

The failure is required for the animal because they are dumber than a vacuum. Animals need explicit instructions that cannot be varied or voided in order to procreate. They could not be given the leeway to do anything but procreate as scripted.

Nature provided the means by which we become an emotionally balanced, loving, giving, human, sentient race.

It is only an animal's instincts that force the man's inability to share orgasm. The animal has those instincts because it hasn't enough sense to engage in procreation without them. Men can easily overcome the instincts of the animal and provide mutual orgasm. Men can think. They can bypass the instincts of the animal. They can also procreate without depending on instincts.

Over a lifetime, the male believes what he has been told by his elders. The insane coverup that men have it all. Slowly (not so slowly nowadays) he begins to realize that he is missing the most important aspect of being human: love. The ache bears him down in hopelessness and, often, the desire for destruction. The older man often lashes out. All unknowingly, it drives him mad.

We just need to get humanity over the hump and become human. I have provided everything to initiate the process. I finally listened to what Nature was telling us. It is not complicated. Future generations that are over the hump of all of the delusions, deceptions, and confusion will take to loving coitus like a fish to water. Aristotle's quote on habits applies.

I have described the situation well enough for any man, even the first generation with all of his built-in fears and avoidance, to comprehend and perform loving coitus. It only takes a few pages, even for the first generation embedded in all the lies, to understand. *If they try. If they put a human effort into understanding*. If they can show some patience and love, they will succeed. The much bigger hurdle is overcoming the deceits that have grown over the millennia to convince him its no use.

Even if it were impossible for men to last as long as she desires, it would be essential for us to quit lying to ourselves. Just be thankful I am so thorough. You're welcome.

There is so much wrong about our existence but it all begins with the male having not learned what is crucial: how to give in bed, learn to love, and become human. The monstrous trail of deception leads back three thousand years.

If you think about that for just a moment, you will begin to realize the ramifications, the massive effect on everything that we accept as reality today. It is everywhere to be seen.

As women attempt to express their love, they (at first) expect it to be returned in equal measure. That is rapidly changing. It doesn't take too long nowadays for them to realize that they are mistaken. Love is returned so seldom from anyone of the male gender. That is creating its own tangential problems. Our awareness of our situation cannot be avoided.

Our awareness of our situation is growing and, yet, we still cannot see through to the obvious conclusion. Instead, we are becoming more convinced of the lies that we have all accepted. Men are hopeless and women are collateral damage.

So far, instead of confidence, instead of self-respect becoming reinforced by the full expression of love, the best men put on their broken smile and keep their nose to the grindstone. Wouldn't it be better if they could all love in full measure?

Self

I have harped on the lack of self-respect, self-confidence, basically the corruption of self-image in both genders, though it is propagated by the male gender's impossible situation of not knowing how to give in bed. Self-respect is the missing trait, the necessity by which all of the other natural noble characteristics of a human, sentient, emotionally balanced, stable, loving race become internalized. There is only one reason it is absent.

In the prehuman state, honesty gives way to self-interest. The loving act turns into selfishness for the male that cannot provide love. Self-respect is abdicated due to self-deceit. The individual acts out the part of a human as long as there is no disturbance. He returns to the animal at the drop of a hat.

With self-respect comes a measure of selflessness. The human is not the animal that Wall Street and economists would like to believe. How far will that selflessness go? Only time will tell. It is certain it won't go so far as to destroy the human race, as we are so glibly doing today.

I mentioned earlier (another new insight) that, not only does the current state of coitus create the selfish persona of the male but it also creates the selfless persona of the woman. This imbalanced state led to misogyny. With love comes equality.

It is not the case that men's lack of giving or loving is due to being dull-witted, somehow mentally incapacitated, or genetically short-changed. It is a physical conundrum that has remained incomprehensible to the male for one reason only: inertia of stupour. Its side-effects ripple out in all directions, including the awful treatment of women and the widespread destruction in which our race so enthusiastically engages.

To gain our stability as a race of sentient beings, this all needs to become common knowledge, part of the Great Conversation.

A few folks creating a loving existence for themselves does little. *The male gender* has to transform itself.

It doesn't even require this book. This book will be helpful to the first generation to 1) overcome the lies and 2) learn how to perform loving coitus.

Later generations will learn how to love easily enough without the lies blocking their progress and a previous generation that has gained its confidence and self-respect through the fulfillment of the physical aspect of loving. Learning the physical elements is simple once the lies no longer block them from consideration.

There will always be more to learn but coitus can finally become a mutually loving engagement for *anyone*, right now.

A new perspective

The distorted reality in which we find ourselves is so far from a sentient reality that it took considerable effort amidst twelve years of near total isolation for me to overcome the miasma of delusions that have been building for three millennia. It has been very much like learning a new language. Attempting to talk to anyone on such a profound, misunderstood topic came out as gibberish. That was the reason for the isolation. I tried a few times to explain. I was so damned certain that one person would understand. I was wrong. The language barrier was too much.

We cannot be human until men, at least, realize and admit that they are lousy at coitus. It just seemed to me crucial to go the extra step and prove that men can be good at coitus. That was not nearly as much effort as overcoming the nonsense.

The lies in which we live are so comprehensive. In essence, though, our dilemma is just so simple - once you get past the lies.

Coitus, in its animal form, is found wanting by a sentient race. That is easily understandable. Coitus, for a sentient race, is meant to be an exchange of giving; a graceful, engaging, elegant, loving enactment of sex that no other animal can attain. It provides a balance between selfishness and selflessness. I have referred to sentient love as an advanced form of caring enabled by the physical aspect of giving by *both* genders.

It took me a lifetime to even find the source, the root cause of our insanity. Most importantly, it was by an unfathomably determined effort to *not* consider all of the crap, all of the surface issues that everyone engages on/focuses on while avoiding the biggest issue: we are not yet human.

The bombardment, urging me to be horrified by all of the little, individual pieces of nonsense and engage in surface issues, was constant. As if attacking them has ever done any good. The general, nonsensical example of this is, "Pick a side", "Spend your time being horrified and attacking the surface issues" that never change a goddamned thing of import in the long run. Become distracted. Media mania is the animal in overdrive.

The problem with all of the nonessential pursuits of surface issues is that they do not move the human race forward an inch. It is all just damage control. It is all just distraction from what is really going on. We have never lost for our missing humanity.

I decided to explore a way to attain our humanity. So, that is the unlikely task that I pursued. I did not expect to succeed.

Instead of even attempting to understanding what was going on, we have heaped insanity on top of insanity - for three thousand years! The animal succeeded at disrupting humanity for that long. It is time to lay the animal to rest permanently, decisively, irrevocably. No more reverting to the snarling animal at the drop of a hat, when things aren't going our way. No more 'losing it'. No more frothing at the mouth.

We did not distinguish a crucial trait regarding our difference from the animal: conscious or sentient awareness. The difference was too subtle for our ancient ancestors to grasp.

Because of sentient awareness we *always* knew that coitus was broken, incomplete, unfulfilled. We tried to run from what we could not seem to change. Awareness is not something that can be denied. It has hunted us down for three millennia.

We cannot avoid the conclusion that coitus, as enacted by an animal, is not enough for a human, though we have spent the last three thousand years attempting to to do. We *act* as if everything is alright, while the elephant is lying on the bed next to you.

Our ability to think grew rapidly without impediment. Our sentient awareness remained blunted. It takes both to overcome our awful state and attain our sanity as well as our humanity. It takes balance. It takes emotional stability and honesty.

It takes an educated heart as well as an educated mind. We lost three thousand years due to inertia and lethargy.

A critical aspect of our existence, sex, was taken for granted initially and we never looked back. It dates back a billion years before humans ever even existed. "That's just the way it is."

It was just something we did. No thought required. No questions asked. In most cases, it came down to one way in which do so. Coitus. Coitus has barely changed in three thousand years. We rut like animals. It began, at some point, to make us uncomfortable *because* of our awareness. Mallananaga (or Pandora's Box) dates our awareness back at least three thousand years. As our awareness has grown, so has the uncomfortable feeling that all is not right regarding sex. It slowly came to the surface against every obstacle we put in its way. We still avoid the obvious conclusion. It is mind-boggling.

Coitus worked, after a fashion. It's just that it has never worked to the extent that our sentient awareness knew was necessary, fully possible, and acceptable *for a sentient race*.

The embarrassing failure, of which men learned to become (unnecessarily and wrongly) ashamed, was suppressed and the immediate damage was to relationships and women. The damage has slowly crept through every aspect of our existence.

Misogyny has a source. It can be cleaned up in a hurry and *naturally* replaced with equality and equitable gender relations. Laws and such will never get us there. They can only highlight the problem. We will hide from the issue until it is gone.

As I have discovered in this book, misogyny is as much about the opposing forces of selfishness drilled into the male versus selflessness accepted by the female. In essence, it is the same as that which I have been saying for a while. Men take and women give and it all starts in bed. I won't explain further.

You should be able to see how men's lack of a loving perspective created misogyny. It's not complicated. Their inadvertent and unnecessary shame and selfishness drove them to prop up their untenable position without mentioning it.

The conundrum of the awful ongoing mistreatment of women is straightforward. Men were ashamed of their failure. The act of taking, without giving, creates selfishness. Men have been so ashamed they despised any mention of it. Sadly, most men have considered it a personal problem, not realizing that it affects the whole length and breadth of the male gender.

They hid from it. We discussed it so little there is no way a man could easily realize it is a common lack.

Women, the perfectly developed sentient creature's very existence, threw it in the faces. Not intentionally. It was just their very loving existence of the woman disturbed the animal that the male remained. He needs to become human.

The rupture in our sentient state began at the beginning.

I hope you know well that I am *not* condoning the awful treatment of women throughout the ages. My rage at the situation remains unquenched. It is what drove me on. I have always wanted to love a woman. Only one aspect was missing.

While, of late, we have really stirred up the dust around sex and the different ways in which it can be accomplished, _have you ever heard mention of anything regarding coitus being inadequate?_ Of course not! It makes babies and the guy gets his rocks off! What else should be expected of coitus??!?!

Let me be precision clear, that is a stupid animal's answer to a human dilemma that we never dared broach or even admit. We fumbled it as our sentience first emerged from animal and never recovered. We accepted that we shouldn't even try. We have just been bamboozled by the inertia of the ongoing stupour.

The question that we should have been asking all along regarding coitus is what should a human, sentient race expect?

The root answer, that leads to the full answer, is so obvious as to be embarrassing. Mutual orgasm. Where does that lead?

It leads in two directions. The first is that men are lousy at coitus because they cannot last long enough to provide mutual orgasm. It is a sentient failure. It is not necessary. Read Details.

The other direction leads to the most important characteristic for humanity that leads to all of the other human, noble characteristics that we have sought for three thousand years without the slightest success. Love. Real, unfiltered, unalloyed love. Nature provided. The dominoes go something like this.

Transformation

All of humanity loses its self-respect when coitus is something best done in the dark. The failure of enacting coitus in a manner consistent with our sentient awareness sends us right back to the animal state. Our intellect goes haywire without an honest assessment of life, when presented with a false reality.

Our intellectual awareness of human virtues (noble traits) is not enough. It needs to be supplemented by the heart's confirmation of those virtues. They need to become internalized.

When orgasms become mutual in the most natural, elegant form of coitus; for which Nature provided the answer for a sentient race that can think, that can overcome instincts, that is human, we will retain our self-respect.

Self-respect leads to the spontaneous development of humanity's noble characteristics (e.g. honour, integrity, honesty, dignity, etc); once self-respect is retained throughout a lifetime and not scuttled at puberty, love wins out. Real, unadulterated, mutually fulfilled love that can expand to encompass the human race is the end result of attaining our sentience. Intimate love that is fulfilled is just the beginning.

The noble characteristics have always been there for the taking. Only the undermined characteristic of self-respect/self-confidence due to the blatant lies that we all have fully accepted have made it impossible to adopt the other naturally occurring characteristics that are so clearly human. They have to become a natural extension of self. They cannot be forced down like cod liver oil. Who can sustain noble characteristics when they don't respect themselves? The lies and fear rule in the meantime.

That success leads to love, or maybe let's say equitable circumstances, on a human wide scale. It is not the flower-throwing, love-you-while-you-bash-me-over-the-head love. It is a real love with substance behind it. That goes well beyond the intimate and successful coupling of two people.

It is the end of the endless cycle of paranoia. It is the end to the very valid belief in the *pre*human monster (signifying nothing). It hasn't been hiding under the bed. It has been in the bed with you. It is not a demon that needs to be exorcised or executed. You can't read it in the Tarot cards. You can't look it up in a medical journal. It is the human race gaining its heart. The human race needs to accept its humanity and respect itself.

Oh, there are probably a dozen other ways, more detailed or taking in different elements to describe the transformation (e.g. education of the heart; love radiating from its source: the intimate relationship between two people that can finally blossom to its full extent and expand beyond the couple, etc).

All the same, it comes down to humanity gaining its emotional stability, honesty, sanity, balance, and ability to love in a rational manner. *That* requires self-respect. *That* requires loving coitus or full admission and certainty that loving coitus is not possible.

If you can ask yourself, what do all of the other forms of sex that are becoming so prevalent provide that coitus doesn't, you will find the answer easily. Mutual orgasm. The difficulty is not arriving at an answer. The difficulty is asking yourself the question. It seems almost a betrayal of the human race.

"Coitus is necessary!!! How could you possibly question its value??!?!" It is *not* a betrayal of a *human, sentient* race. It is liberation from the animal. It is admitting that animals always fumbled at coitus. The animal rendition of coitus is not complete. The animal's rutting behaviour suits an animal. It does not suit a human. If all we could get out of it was babies, then we should know it with certainty. I have presented why that is not the case. I have proved it to myself. I am not superhuman, so I am certain others can learn. Before long, it will be as easy as riding a bike.

Burying the question for at least three thousand years was the betrayal of our humanity. Whether we could make it better or not, the deceit ruined us for three millennia.

We always assumed we were too stupid to overcome the animal's limitations or, at least, face the failure. That is a travesty that knows no bound. Asking the question is liberation from the animal that has always had its claws in our back.

No, I'm sorry to say, pills taken by the billions per year do not resolve the issue. That does not lead to the restoration of the male's self-respect, end to his shame, or feelings of inadequacy. It does not remove his toxic masculinity. If anything, it amplifies it, makes it more concrete.

Suffice it to say that it is easy to make coitus into a loving engagement of two people without pills, appliances, or acrobatics. Coitus *can make love*. All explained in Details.

Hell, cunnilingus is better than pills. At least, it is honest.

The most intimate form of love is not created, not fulfilled, until the orgasms become mutual. We *make* love when the orgasms are mutual. We *create* love by *making* love. The phrase 'making love' was *not* accidental.

Suffice it to say that *making* love *requires* mutual giving, mutual orgasm, mutual pleasure, mutual satisfaction. We are not human until that is the case, however it is accomplished. Mutual orgasm *makes* love by ending the selfish/selfless disparity. The lack of sharing orgasm destroys any attempt at creating real, fulfilled love. It requires the man to hide his shame and the woman to accept the unacceptable.

Making love creates an equal basis for both genders and, hence, you guessed? Equality and equitable status for the woman, *at last*. The man's self-respect, *at last*. A fully *shared* journey through life.

No more need to rule by fear. Note the origins of that rule by fear. It is the fear that men have carried with them since the beginning. The fear of failure that has always rode them like a burr under the saddle. Rule by fear became the standard instead of love. In some ways, it is the tale of two genders of animal attempting to become human.

No more, the attempts to expose individual, isolated incidents of the misogyny that could never solve the problem. It is not isolated, individual incidents. It is a perfect example of taking a surface issue approach to a much deeper problem. We try to identify individual cases but never look to see the big picture. Misogyny is a gender-wide phenomenon with few exceptions. That is the only way it could exist the way it does. I guess, in some ways, it was the highlighting of the awfulness of misogyny's individual acts that led to the deeper answer.

When the noble traits develops internally, no outside force can dislodge them. When the awfulness of the situation is exposed, the lies just goes underground, noble traits ignored. It is internalized rather than our humanity. Our humanity needs to develop internally.

There are a lot of reasons that the issue of coitus is at the heart of all of our troubles. Let's start with the simplest.

Coitus is at the heart of the ongoing existence of our race and, also, at the heart of the majority of intimate relationships. It is repeated (thrown in our faces, if you will) on nearly a daily basis. At least, until the misery takes over and the couple no longer bothers. The relationship suffers when coitus remains an animal's act. The suffering expands from its source. It affects all within purview before it is over.

As I mention above, you will never hear a complaint about coitus being inadequate. That underlines one of the worst aspects of the situation. We all know it. It is used as a line in so many comedies. Researchers have built their careers on studying it. And, yet, we never really talk about it.

Honesty is *necessary.* Self-respect enables it. Fear destroys it. Selfishness destroys honesty as it seeks deceit as a coverup.

I want to emphasize a subtle piece that I have tried to convey before. It feels like a lot of repetition because it is difficult to explain so many pieces buried beneath so many lies. I hope future generations can do a better, more precise job.

Love is a sentient trait. It is *the* sentient trait. Self-respect enables the other noble characteristics that are humanity's for the taking. Love is the all-encompassing trait. One can think of love as the bundling of the other *human* traits into one word.

Love will not stop at loving one other individual intimately. It has to proliferate into a trait *shared* across the human race.

How to explain? Rather than the suspicious look that is so often encountered, rather than the begrudging acceptance of the stranger (or not), rather than the paranoid delusions regarding anyone that is not a complete duplicate of you, humanity opens its arms to all. Shocking idea, right?

Let me try to explain it with less flowery/poetic imagery.Love, the feeling of oneness that *can be* shared between a man and a woman, will radiate outward. Once the home becomes an abode of love, it will radiate outward and interlink.

Yeah, still kinda flowery, right? It's my rhoetic bug. Let's try this. Rather than the split personality that severs prehumanity into many little opposing, often violent pieces, humanity will accept itself. Love will be seen on the face and deliberations of every individual that lives amongst a race of humans that has its self-respect because it *know* the tremendous fulfillment of physical love, whose resultant self-respect is sustained. There seems to be no in-between for me. Poetic or *anal*ytical.

I need to stress this, also. There will be some (though it may be very few) that, either through choice (though that seems unlikely), lack of opportunity, or other circumstance, don't participate in the physical loving exchange. That is not really important. Their confidence that, if and when presented with the gift, they will succeed, will be enough. Self-respect, today, is torn to pieces before the final coup de grace of failure of coitus. It is instilled since birth through the paradigms saying they are not worthy, that they are nothing more than a demented animal.

In the same way, self-respect will become a natural birthright when it has no reason to become undermined. It can be nurtured from birth rather than torn to pieces. Thus, while the joy of the loving exchange may be absent for some few, the noble characteristics will remain in place. One can say it rubs off on others when there is no impediment. Or, it is self-sustaining.

Deceits

We fumbled our first attempts at understanding coitus. Hell, even animals may know it. *They just can't verbalize it.* We have lied to ourselves throughout our existence *because* we could not admit this. *We have never verbalized it. We suppressed it.*

We are not natural liars. It is conditioned into us as we avoided *one subject*. *The one subject that is unavoidable.* The one subject that we enact repeatedly throughout or lives, in one form or another. Sentient awareness desires clarity. Always. We are built for honesty We misled ourselves from the start.

Think of it this way. We come along and attempt to verbalize the perplexing situation. It goes against our grain to lie but it is either that or admit that coitus is broken with no *apparent* resolution. It was too important that coitus continue. It was too much for our early ancestors to contend with. So, they lied. They concocted stories in desperation to assure that we would continue to couple and make babies. "Sex is only for making babies!", they proclaim. We reinforced those stories to the extent that it is nearly impossible to see through to the truth.

I have gone into detail in each of the books on all of this attempting to make it clear. Our sentient awareness wants nothing more than a straight story. Does that get it across?

We don't like to lie but we have been taught all along the way to lie. All because of one lie that rests at the heart of all relationships, all of our existence. It is never mentioned and it stalks us every day. It is the lie that deceived the heart rather than educate it. We were taught to avoid the thought at all costs.

Even without loving coitus, it would be critical that the lie be put away and the truth, that mutual orgasm makes for equality and equitable treatment, be acknowledged.

There is plenty of evidence that we are most interested in telling the truth. We only lied in the desperation of a witless animal. We are no longer a witless animal. Our sentience has been pounding away at the truth for three millennia.

Even worse, though, are the massive ramifications of the lie.

Can you even admit to yourself why coitus is inadequate? The reason we have lied about it for so long? Without quaking? In this context, it brings into focus much more.

If you look at each new generation, especially over the last century or so, they have rebelled against what is going on. This emphasizes just how well the *actual* problem is buried.

Essentially, our existence is not human and everybody knows it. We just have never been able to pinpoint the problem. Our minds *always* veer away from the contemplation.

The desire to seek resolution is pummeled out of each of us over a lifetime by disappointment and tricks of the animal that remains in charge.

It is no wonder that, as a generation begins to perceive what is going on, they are appalled. They can't help it. Their sentient awareness cannot be denied - until it is thoroughly pummeled out of them and hammered home by the all-encompassing failure of coitus to meet sentient expectations without explanation.

What needs to be highlighted, though, is that *it is right there in front of us and, yet, **we never ever say, "Hey, the lack of loving coitus is LOUSY!!!!** It is truly mind-boggling!

Can you see the disparity? Men want sex but can't make it attractive to the woman without alternative methods. So, the unfulfilled woman loses interest over a lifetime. All of the youthful promise of life is lost. All of the alternatives are better than the lack of mutual orgasm. But, none can compare to coitus. Looking into your lover's eyes as each reaches climax is special.

It is also no wonder that the previous generation, over a lifetime, comes to accept that there is nothing to be done. Alternatives are rejected. It has been pummeled into them. They eventually embrace their misery and call it home.

So, what is the younger generation rebelling against, specifically? No one has really ever known. They just know that something is seriously wrong. More seriously with each new generation. We call it matters like 'freedom' and 'liberty'. Really? Freedom and liberty *from what?* Most have a great deal of liberty and, still, they are miserable. It doesn't add up until you realize we want freedom from the animal.

The Flower Power, or 'Free Love', generation let it rain. LGBTQ opened the floodgates.

It has been going on for much longer than that. Simone de Beauvoir is my favorite past heroine of the search for sanity and suspicions regarding sex, love, and the genders. And, Freud before her. Many, many more have attempted to understand the complexity of something that spans our complete existence from before history ever began.

There can be no love, no deep abiding caring, if the orgasm is not mutual. How could there be? The self has never been fulfilled, for either gender. There can be affection, if both the man and the woman surrender themselves. That is not love in its fullest form. It is an animal's attempt at caring.

I have tried to stress in my later books, as it became clearer exactly what is going on. *No one*, man or woman, likes the situation the way it is. Neither is fulfilled, neither is *fully* satisfied, when *both* are not fulfilled by the sexual act. Both remain miserable. It is like a gaping hole in our sentient landscape that we have painted out of the picture.

It is just insane that we have never talked about it openly!

The following is another aspect of the deceit that makes it apparent just how deceived we have been, how damaging it has been, and just how urgent an answer has become.

Men finally have begun to attempt to 'investigate'. The investigations themselves are an utter travesty. All the investigations do are confirm and justify the failure that need not exist!

The starting point for all *male* investigations into the matter starts from the standpoint that lasting two or three minutes is the best that can be expected. He should be proud!(?) No one should expect anything better. Really? For an animal, yes. For a human? Let's get real. Let's get human. Let's put away the befuddled, awful animal and begin to use our brains, enabled by our heart's desire.

Keep clearly in mind that it usually takes up to *fifteen to twenty minutes* for a woman to achieve orgasm. We have accepted something that is off by an *order of magnitude* from that which is the *necessary* goal to ever be successful and loving in the most elegant, graceful manner possible. Controlled ejaculation is the only way for coitus to become a loving event.

The only real point of lasting more than a few seconds is to *make love*, which means lasting as long as *she* desires.

Does that shock you? Does it scramble your brain? It shouldn't. It is easily done *by a human*. Instead, we proclaim the goal (or is it gaol?) is two minutes and call it good. Do you see the subtle (maybe not so subtle) hand of misogyny in this? It is so much more than just laziness on the male gender's part, though laziness is one of many results. Does this help you see how misogyny will end when men learn to love in the most magnificent way possible?   The heart of the lie is right there. Can you see how it twists the man like a pretzel?

There is an article in Wikipedia that clearly states that it is a *mystery* why men cannot last longer!!!!!!!!   That is a sure sign of just how thoroughly the animal remains in charge.

The only mystery is why it has taken us three millennia to realize that *we are not just animals!   We can think!!!!!*   We can see past our stupour, defeatism, and surrender.   As humans finally begin to look around, they will realize that we have never really thought about anything.   The stupour caused us to run from ourselves, from contemplating the human reality.

We have always convinced ourselves that there was a time limit, a clocking ticking away.   That was the first mistake.   The second was pegging it at two minutes but that doesn't really matter.   The first mistake matters more than you can yet imagine.

My definition of erectile dysfunction means lasting anything less than as long as *she* desires.   For a human, that is.   A pill is no solution.   It is an animal's crutch.   It does not make us human.

We have never even explored the idea of *indefinitely delayed* or *controlled* ejaculation at all.   How can that possibly be?   Over three thousand years, no one ever thought, "gee, maybe we can last as long as *she* pleases.   Maybe I can last as long as is *necessary!* without all the hubbub."?

It's not even on our radar.   That confirms just how severely inadequate coitus (rutting coitus, that is) has messed with our minds.   The mistake dates back a billion years, essentially. Animals can't do better so how could we expect to do so?

In that context, it becomes clear. *DUH!   Because we are not just animals!*   To make it a little clearer, the problem is that we accepted some animal instincts, in other words, something that is done *without thinking*, as if it were immutable rather than just something that a conscious human can change by paying attention!   By thinking!!

The crucial aspect that must be fully understood is the effect it has had on men's behaviour and mental make-up.   It is seen in the way women have been mistreated throughout the ages.   It is seen in the 'camaraderie' of men when they get together and talk about their exploits and their derogatory references to women.   It is seen in the emotional instability of the male gender.   All of the toxic behaviour that turns our existence on its head is all due to compensation for the failure that shouldn't even exist.

Miserable men curling up in a ball never to emerge is an alternative behaviour. The stoic man is another. None are human, loving, emotionally balanced, rationally sentient. One way or another, they are coping with their failure.

It is seen in the insane actions of Torquemada, which are making a comeback (again! for the umpteenth time!). It is seen in the desire to distract that begins with shouting to drown out the truth and ends with violence in just about every form.

Every way in which misogyny is expressed, every way in which we learned to lie, every insanely violent action, every stupoured point of view, interaction, or proclamation all comes back to male compensation for their *unnecessary* lack. Or, if you are *still* questioning whether men can last as long as she desires, then it is due to the deceit that men have been hiding from since the very beginning. Master's of the Universe of Delusion.

The male's self-respect is lacking because of this failure alone. *It is not some genetic failure.* It is not born into men. Males are not born with a lack of self-respect, noble characteristics, unstable emotions, and a limp willie. They are not born the awful creatures that they become. It is a learned response since birth for every man that is reinforced constantly by the previous generation of deluded males. All of the preconditioning is confirmed as he attains puberty and finds himself lacking.

That nails his heart (and his mouth) shut. It may take a few years to catch up to him but it always nails his heart shut. The instincts that cause him to fail dwell deep but they are just instincts, not genetic coding. The toxic behaviour does not dwell deep at all. A generation can dispense with them in a heartbeat.

Because of the conditioning of the ages, a man is somewhat prepared to compensate for his lack by the bluster of his male elders to which he is indoctrinated, imprinted, more surely than the imaginary clock that haunts him throughout his life.

Because of that preparation, it may take a while for it all to hit home for him. That is why you will see so many males slowly become bitter old men as the scam finally hits home - to some extent. They buy nice cars to compensate for their lack or find a young, inexperienced woman that knows no better.

Everybody tries to be honest with themselves. It's just difficult because of the delusions and deceits that we have endured for three thousand years! It is all around us through every day of our lives. We are trained up since birth to accept the awful results.

It was a long road to an honest assessment of what is really going on. I remain infuriated that it had to come down to me to explain. I had also been trained into the nonsense all too well.

Everybody tries to honest with themselves. That includes men, the poor saps. *Everything* going back at least three millennia was concocted to keep us in the dark. No conspiracy theory, just a comedy of errors. A very sad comedy for all.

Sentient awareness, above all, desires truth. It has been fed lies. Our sentient awareness has been held hostage in our subconscious by the burden of lies we have told ourselves in desperation regarding a phantom flaw that never really existed.

I have often wondered whether relationships would do better, once we learn to love. Our prehuman state convinces us that everybody is going to want to sleep around. I was on the fence as to whether this will remain true until lately.

Now, I am certain. In part, I am convinced beyond almost any doubt by the realization that everybody tries to be honest with themselves. Amidst all of the lies brought on by the initial lie, honesty becomes severely compromised.

We feel we have betrayed ourselves and our mate long before anyone actually betrays their mate with an affair. The lack of mutual orgasm and coital bliss is the initial betrayal. We become so compromised that we cannot tell truth from lie. 'Anything goes' once honesty is thrown out the window with fervor.

It seems t o me love between a couple should easily last a lifetime for most, if not all, couples. Everyone only runs around because they never feel satisfaction, fulfillment.

It is like an unfed hunger for the fulfillment of loving coitus. The man feels he has betrayed the woman the first time he takes her to bed. The woman may feel betrayed as well (not my place to say; and, once again, I must mention that the woman seems to feel betrayed by the change of character of the male as his lack hits home for him, maybe much more than lack of orgasm for some (those that never experience orgasm would be my guess)). So, an affair is a small matter. The betrayal already happened.

It may take some time for the adjustment to take place (that can be said of every aspect of overcoming the debacle of the ages), but it seems relationships should mostly last a lifetime, sooner or later. Sooner, I hope, of course.

Sex Objects

Here's where it gets tricky. A misconception that has confused us down through the ages is the seemingly accepted reason why men only see women as only a sex object.

The erroneous belief is that men have sexual needs that drive them to find sexual release/relief. It's not an erroneous belief that men are driven by sexual relief. The misconception is that it is the root cause of the problem.

I've always thought that one of the worst jokes ever is that so many men want a steady woman because they want steady sex and, yet, that seldom obtains.

The man, as well as the woman, finally admit to themselves, sooner or later, that he is failing and he hates himself all the more. Unless he is one of the rare individuals that finds some way to please the woman, whether it is coitus or some other effort, there is some form of backlash, from a morose relationship, to affairs, to domestic violence.

The male *never sees what he is missing* because he is not yet human. He will never see what is behind that beautiful, incredible body until the act of coitus becomes love-making. Thus, she becomes a sex object, a necessity, not a gift. Someone that will tolerate his lousy attempts at coitus.

Men have to learn to care about the woman, the human. He has to give in bed in order to do so. He is blinded by his failure to love and becomes selfish. He just takes and takes and takes.

Men seek only sex because they cannot achieve love. They cannot achieve love because they cannot fulfill the woman physically. They insidiously *learn* not to give. Can you see this? How this cripples and blinds the man to his humanity and love? It is all an act of 'taking'; capture, conquer, charm, seduce; none of it is an act of love, of giving. It is the sham of the animal.

In today's prehuman world, love never stood a chance without the realization that love is far more than we have ever understood. What we consider love is a watered-down, paltry sum.   A lifetime of an intimate, loving relationship rarely happens.   Do not confuse this with a lifetime of tolerance, mundanity, bitter feelings, and acceptance of misery.

That honest streak is in everyone of us. It comes with sentient awareness. It cannot be avoided. It drives us mad when ignored. A mind that has our form of awareness *has to* try to correlate what it senses to what it comprehends. Existence requires an *honest* explanation for a sentient being.

Men only act out the part.   We play the part of lover and human being. It is impossible for the man to develop a cohesive internal structure for all of the reasons I have been highlighting.

My streak of honesty is so thoroughly unsuppressed, so in charge of my life, that I couldn't *ever* tolerate *acting* like a lover. I have always wanted to love a woman. I could not just act out the part. Which was the best I could do until way too late in life. I damn well wanted to *be* that lover, not act out the part.

Our trait of honesty becomes suppressed over a lifetime because of the deceit at the heart of our very existence. Put on an act for this. Put on an act for that. Where is the real human? It becomes lost in the fray that signifies nothing.

Willpower is a poor substitute for love. All of this will only change when love becomes the common denominator of our humanity.

Sometimes I wonder if it is really necessary to explain how love will transform our existence like nothing that has ever come before. Changing from neanderthal to our human form does not even begin to compare.   That is a blip on the animal's radar compared to fulfilled human loving. That will change us into a fulfilled sentient race. It makes us sane, balanced, emotionally stable, rational, *and human*. The *pre*human will be gone to dust with one hundred years, once we get off our duffs.

The Woman's Perspective

I have always pondered why women cannot get what I am saying. It just seems like it should be so obvious for a woman.

Whatever the real reason, a number of possible concerns present themselves. Since I have never gotten a straight answer, I have had to guess.

The skepticism that seems most likely is that some believe there is no way that *all* men will learn how to love. A key point that it is no more difficult *for a human* than learning to ride a bike are walk. Also, a point is that no man likes failing at the most essential act of human life. I think that answers, if that is a concern. If it is within reach, any man will jump at the chance.

I've mentioned one concern ad nauseam. The change in a man's behaviour is what really irks women. I am not sure that many women are able to accept that men are not naturally assholes. It is highly likely it is considered a genetic trait.

This, as well as others, falls into the category of 'we believe what we believe', no matter the truth. Perception as reality.

I think the growing realization that may or may not have always been there, to some extent, is that she too can experience orgasm. Those that know this, don't tolerate nearly as much nonsense from the males or play them like a fiddle. I wonder if some women worry about losing that leverage. I'll just say that the leverage is part and parcel with misogyny.

There is one I have sensed from many women. Because the man cannot last long enough, the woman feels that it is her fault. That she is not attractive enough or who know? Just like the man, she does not realize it is a common problem *for men*. It is never the woman's problem.

That whole mess, of course, breaks my heart but, this one, in particular, tramples it. The deceit is turned against the woman. Just like The Garden Of Eden. Keep her in her place.

Another is that a woman may think, "Omigoodness! Whickwithy is going to create a world of monsters strutting around wanting to show off how good they are at coitus. He's going to create a world of Don Juans!"

Here's the thing. When every man is Don Juan, no man is Don Juan. They are, then, a loving man. It won't impress a woman if a particular man is good at sex when they all are. So, a woman won't fall for any strutting male. That is, of course, only a small part of the vast change that will happen.

Toxic masculinity might be another concern?   "Is this, somehow, just a man excusing the male gender?" I don't really think anyone believes this. Toxic manhood is nothing more than men compensating for their lack, because they are scared little boys, ashamed of their failure at fulfilling the promise of love in the most important act of being a loving human. They act as if they are to blame. That is just as wrong. It is just that they remain a herd of animals always following someone's lead. I *think* I have been pretty clear. Once they fulfill love, they become human. I don't know. Maybe some don't believe that?

Mostly because I don't believe I have explained it as well as I should, I *can* imagine a lot of women saying, "It takes more than just lasting forever. If I am bored, I am bored. No matter how long he keeps thrusting."

True enough, but all of the rest of loving and caring is easy, *once the man learns he won't fail!* The finer points *are* something that comes naturally once the man is naturally human. If he is not shunting his brain into the void, he will pay attention to the woman he engages. That is just another aspect of love. He will, of course, seek what else is missing (if anything is). The man is stunted in so many ways when he knows he will fail. It comes out especially clear in his lack of the art of loving. It is an embarrassment for him, start to finish, until he knows he can succeed. He is a dispirited wreck until that happens.

Here' the one that really blows me away to contemplate. Is it possible that some women say, "This is all about men. As if they were the center of the universe." I sure hope not. If so, I have really missed the boat. This is attempting to circumvent that exact ludicrous delusional grandeur of men that *is only compensation for their failure!*

Another, which I have heard from young women, is, "I don't need no damn orgasm. I love my man." Yeah, tell me that, again, when you are forty or fifty and have wasted your life and your potential for love, when the lack leads to disinterest in sex for the woman and the man is still raging for sex. That is pure witless conditioning.

Is there the possibility that women will still not desire sex as often as the man, even if they achieve full-on orgasm? I guess it is possible. We won't know until the woman achieves full-on orgasm regularly from her intimate relationship with a man. I don't expect that to be the case.

Informed innocence

We are at a discontinuity. The naive innocence of the animal continues to be trampled. We are getting to the point that we are ready to just give up and thrash around like we are no more than an overly intelligent animal, which is all we are today. We treat the concept of innocence as if it were a shame.

We treat innocence as if it were a burden rather than an essential component of sentient life. Heck, any life. Our animal innocence was trampled as soon as we tried to hide from what our sentient awareness was telling us. It doesn't suit us.

We require informed innocence. In the short term, it will also require armour against the nonsense. It has yet to take the place of the naive innocence of the animal.

There is quite a distance left between attaining our informed, armoured innocence and abandoning the armour.

We must change course and realize that all of our dreams were accurate. Humanity really can be much more than political correctness matched against insanity and bombs. Sex can be more than just rutting. Love can be real.

It begins with a clear interpretation of events and removal of the single deception that has derailed us for millennia.

Make no mistake. As long as coitus continues to be enacted as an animal, it will remain a disaster. But, the most crucial disaster is the lies we have told ourselves from the start.

Informed innocence is provided by an unobstructed perception of what is really going on from a sentient perspective. It is a crucial component of sentient awareness. It is not naive. It is not gullible. It is an honest assessment of reality without the countless awful distortions we have thrown in.

What is perceived by our sentient awareness has to make sense. It has to correlate. Our sense of truth needs to be unburdened by all of the paradigms of nonsense and deceit that we developed as we crawled out of our caves.

The split personality needs to become one. The pessimist and the optimist, the practical and the dreamer, the selfishness and selflessness, need to become one, not two factions fighting for supremacy. No more "Pick a side" based on foolish vague answers that answer nothing of import.

We need to accept that the universe is, at worst, indifferent and benign. We need to become human. This only happens once we retain our self-respect. We can then perceive reality with clarity.

Informed innocence is only something that can be sustained as a race with an unobstructed, sentient perspective. It has to become part of the human mindset. Clarity must prevail for the human race to attain its humanity and end the foolish split personality, the stupour, the endless violence, and destruction. Only then, will informed innocence lose its armour.

Informed innocence realizes that the universe is okay. It's just the demented version of the sentient animal called human that causes havoc due to its paranoid antics developed by an animal outside of its comfort zone. It is crucial that we understand why we became demented, deceitful, paranoid, and delusional. Humanity, a fully aware sentient being, can only be comfortable in the full regalia of its sentient awareness.

It is not naïveté. It is not gullibility. Informed innocence flourishes when the reigning sentient species is sane.

It isn't that an informed innocent is unequipped or unaware of the potential for havoc. They just don't need to spend an inordinate amount of time contemplating the possibility. The one source of constant havoc - a demented sentient race will be gone.

Gullibility and naïveté are non-sequiturs in such a situation. "Fool me once" only obtains when someone is committed to using another as a fool.

I am not even sure if it is possible for a fully equipped human to lose its innocence and self-respect without it all being undermined before its sentient faculties have developed. Today, it all comes crashing down at puberty after a constant assault of paradigms of nonsense during prepubescence.

Maturity, today, seems to be defined as losing one's innocence. "Wise up to the monstrous world in which you live". I beg to differ. Wake up and overcome the monstrous prehumanity that creates all of the havoc. Quit acting like you are just an animal. Live the dream. Gain your sentient innocence. And, sooner or later, shed the armour.

The road forward

As we continue to fight the realization that coitus, *in its incomplete, incompetent, inept, inane, inadequate, inattentive animal rendition*, is not suitable for humans, the stupour continues to deepen and the split personality becomes schizoid.

Any form of *mutual orgasm* is better than that. But, loving coitus is incomparable. It is also indispensable for procreation. Once we achieve loving coitus as the only form of coitus, we will release our sentient awareness and become human. I am not sure anything short of that can do the same.

This does not discount all of the other forms of mutual orgasm in which humanity engages. It is just that loving coitus is the most elegant, natural form. Humanity will always *require* coitus.

To me, the defining characteristic of loving coitus is that one has the great joy of looking into the eyes of their lover as they experience transcendence. And, of course, it makes babies. That's kinda important. Why should coitus suffer another day from being less than a loving effort?

The evidence of its importance is clearly seen in the maniacal way in which its lack has been suppressed. The inability of humanity to admit that there is anything wrong with coitus as enacted by an animal says it all. 'Maniacal' is an accurate term and defines our current state. It is not a coincidence.

Twelve years. Twelve fucking years and I'm still getting to the bottom of it all. That is just how deep the stupour is that we have embraced with all of our will for three thousand years. When will the human race begin to awaken to its sentient awareness? When will it finally put away all of the animal's foolishness? When will the truth become something more than a laughable phrase that everyone shirks? How long will we shun our humanity. I am beginning to wonder if there is time left for humanity to gain its humanity.

Centerpiece

We have always thought of change as something that must be forced - with laws, restrictions, etc. Change that is forced on the individual can never work for a sentient race. It cannot transform humanity into something more than an animal. It is a prehuman, demented animal's attempt to make things work - for an animal. The animal remains when the insights are forced.

Civilized. An interesting word. Laws attempt to force us to *act* civil. That is a far cry from *being* human and loving.

The change that counts has to come from within. Or, more exactly, not a change but a continuity of sanity throughout a person's life, a growing emotional stability that begins from within the person at birth due to growing self-confidence and self-respect in its human environment. I can never leave out self-respect when I explain this, because some pompous fool will talk about how confident he is. While his lack of substantial confidence may not be plain to see, lack of self-respect is clear. His lack of humanity is stark.

Most precisely, the rot that eats away at men comes from within. There is only one way that the rot does not continue to fester. 'Toughen up' is an animal's quip. It can never work. The rot does not magically disappear. It just grows without self-respect and a growing confidence in humanity.

Our humanity comes from an existence that is compatible with the human, sentient awareness. The state that we cannot avoid and have been way too afraid to fulfill. Setting rules to be nice while continuing to suffer is only training a person to mimic Pavlov's Dog. He will turn and bite you at a moment's notice.

Maybe the best description of our mess is that we are all playacting around the fact that coitus is broken. Everything we do is influenced by our past inability to make coitus work for humanity and adamant avoidance of that admission.

We all know it. It is as obvious as the sun rising. Yet, we act like that's the way it should be for a human *for no good reason*. That deceit continues to blind and baffle our sentient awareness.

Even if it remained a failure, we would have to own up to it openly to progress into a human state.

Is it impossible for so many to believe that we don't have to be such a colossal failure as a race? The failure itself is clear to all.

We took the template that the female gender represents and tried to force fit it to the male animal. The male animal needs to *become* human, not act out the part.

Look around. We have tried to train the male animal for more than three thousand years without the slightest iota of success.

Concocting and believing in imaginary gods set us back millennia. It takes something more. It takes men learning to give in the most essential physical expression of love. It takes men gaining their self-respect. It takes men owning up to their failure. They need to learn to *be* human, not just act out the part. To do so, they need to learn to give, they need to learn to love.

Trajectory of Nature

Before humanity, Nature relied on genetics for the next improvement in life, the next step in evolution. Now, with the advent of humanity, it is relying on sentient awareness. It is a tremendous change.

The idea of game theory suggests that a win-win situation is *always* better. It is as if it is part of Nature's plan, Nature's trajectory. Nature's long-term intent seems to be to get around the dead-end of selfishness. Love seems to apply. With sentient awareness, Nature is attempting to improve into a win-win situation. That situation begins when both the man and the woman *win* in bed. Until that happens, the animal state is replicated in toto. The man tries to convince himself that he has won, but he always knew better. The pompous male act proves the case of his miserable condition and existence.

When both the man and the woman give, finally, a true win-win situation begins to present itself. From this standpoint, the evolution of sentient awareness is far greater than even I have suggested and I have suggested a *lot*. It seems a plan much more subtle, elegant, and fulfilling than any of the bizarre self-aggrandizing gods that prehumans concocted.

I have said before that shouting the phrase "Peace is good" and "Love is good" in no better than saying "War is necessary". They are all just mouthing of phrases that have no import.

Innocence And Signposts
or, The Eyes Of A Child

This is a little bit about the micro-trajectory of *human* life (as opposed the prehuman condition and the macro trajectory of all of life, of living existence).

In my own case, I found that to become a man, from the disrupted state of a male sentient animal stuffed full of preconditioning and bitter feelings after a lifetime of living the scam, it required that I tear myself back down to the barest components of childhood and build it back up into a man. In order to do so, I had to isolate myself from all of the false pretenses of prehumanity in order to reconstruct into something resembling a human. Of course, it can only go so far on my own and, thereby, remain incomplete in this lifetime.

I believe I have been somewhat successful at the attempt as long as I can ignore my age. I hope any man reading this book will find it easier and less arduous than the complete tear-down I had to endure, all on my own, with no help or guidance.

In regards to the micro-trajectory of attaining our sentient state in full, I would like to do some fleeting scenario planning to some extent. I would like to suggest some signposts (as the term is used in scenario planning) to highlight our progress towards our sentient human state. As the landmarks appear, we will know we are getting closer to our humanity.

Grace, elegant behaviour, compassion, sentient innocence and a smile, or the eyes of a child, seem the most useful guideposts. When we see these begin to appear as the general characteristics of humanity, rather than the exception, I think we can say we are well on our way, finally.

Maybe less discernible would be the noble characteristics, such as honesty, self-assurance, honour, integrity, dignity. The characteristics we have never attained.

Much, much farther away down the road to our sanity is the day that no one desires to lead or be led. That will be a change so significant, so implicative of many other changes, that I think we will be able to safely consider ourselves fully human.

Somewhere in between, we will learn to think for ourselves. I would guess this would be one of the first significant transitions. It will be wrenching. Right now, it is consistently more like monkey see, monkey do. I could give endless examples. Maybe I am, once again, overestimating prehumanity but the examples are all around, so I won't bother with any examples.

All of it starts with love in its fullest, intimate, physical form and the end to the falsehood that has held us ransom.

A sentient perspective is the *only* reality; all else is a delusional, deceitful act to compensate for the pain of not achieving the sentient state; an attempt to protect oneself and convince oneself that it is all okay, even as the world burns; such as the interpretation that darkness is light and light is darkness or mankind must remain a brute. Accepting such is surrender to the animal with no human intervention. The sense of self is lost amongst the flotsam of the animal. Yes, this paragraph is a particular form of double entendre with intent.

I'm afraid I indulged the poet in me in this section. Sorry about that. Nero was not the exception. He is the rule.

Sentient awareness

We have hobbled our sentient awareness. We stuffed it into the subconscious as if it were unimportant. The animal guards over the cage constantly. Without sentient awareness to balance our intellect, we remain a demented animal.

I am becoming more and more convinced that sentient awareness is reliant on articulation and elucidation.

This explains why we have so little sentient awareness left after *not* dealing with the appallingly apparent, critically important, problem of the animal's inept enactment of coitus for three millennia.

We never talk about it. We shunted it into the race's subconscious with a vengeance because we could not overcome the failure, bless any alternative or, most importantly, admit to the situation. That has torn us apart and continues to do so.

What makes it utterly frustrating to me is the revelations I describe in Details. We only fooled ourselves due to the stupour.

Even worse, because it is so important to us and because we will not talk about it, over the millennia, the lack of wit the situation causes has deformed everything else we do. We remain dumbfounded due to the most important act of life remaining an indiscernible failure, an accepted misery, an unsuspected tie to the animal that upheaves all of Nature's attempts to make something more out of us - until now.

The suggestion I make is that the claim that we only use 10% of our brain is wrong. We use 90% contending with all of the lies and fallout from this failure. It is a a game of dodgeball with our humanity at stake.

Once the failure is gone, we will recover the use of the rest of our brain. Then, all bets are off. Even my most outrageous suggestions may be well short of the truth of our potential.

The Time Bomb

The more I consider and study the missing 90% of our brain that is used up with contending with the refuse and droppings left behind by the animal, the clearer it becomes.

We spend a great deal of our time sorting through and justifying the utter nonsense lurking in our heads. It was the first attempt at rationalization, otherwise known as lying dressed up to make it pretty.

The surface issues that I mention often are the least part of it. It is the considerations that never see the light of day that tell the real story. The miserable confusions that lay hidden in our minds never to be admitted. We veer away from our sentience awareness and consideration of the real human dilemma.

There's the obvious one: the confounding subject of sex. There's another done, metaphorically, in the dark. Masturbation.

Again, I have to emphasize, why would it take us three thousand years to admit that orgasms are good? That masturbation would be a great way to take care of it, if we weren't utterly ashamed of it? More evidence that the situation has been derailed for so very long that it occurred before words.

It is not as good as sharing the orgasmic event with another but it is far better than going insane avoiding orgasm - which is never the case for a man and, I would guess, seldom the case for the woman. At least, most women I have ever known. But, still, we are unwilling to admit to the case! It is done in the dark.

Murmurs

Beyond the obvious improvements in the human condition that I have explained in detail, once we learn to love, this convinces me that there is even more to it. All of the blatantly awful acts of prehumanity, the lies and dimwittedness that pervade our existence should lessen radically but that is just a speck of dust in the cosmos. I'm not sure how to explain the significance further, so let me just say, this is **_big_** and leave it at that.

There is something about verbalization, articulation. Putting it out there makes it real. It forces itself onto our sentient consciousness, reorienting it. Otherwise, as is the case with all of the ramifications of failing to make coitus into a human endeavor across the board, it creeps stealthily into a position to tear sentient awareness apart from the inside out.

Can you see how it is like a child acting like it broke daddy's watch but doesn't want to admit it? First of all, there should be no shame regarding lousy coitus. That is the way it was given to us. The only real important issue is how we overcome the lack of love that the lack of loving coitus causes. We must not hide from it because we are not human yet.

We have used every trick in the book to make sure the conscious realization that we have been lousy at coitus never took hold. It scared us silly because, without coitus, the human race would be extinct. We need to realize there is more to the story and hiding from it like a child will never make us human.

Along with sentient awareness came expectations. Like the expectation that coitus should be so much more. Or, in general terms, if you like, that humanity could attain love.

In case you are under any delusions, we haven't attained a loving state yet. All of the clamour and din of human life is caused by our certainty that there is something more against the failure to make it so. Love, to an extent that we have hardly been able to imagine, awaits.

It is all just a foolish actor on a stage until we become human. The actor is nothing but a poorly-trained animal playing the part that sentience tells it is human. The dancing bear. A tale told by an idiot.

The Big One: Sentient awareness

The real magic of human existence is the sentient awareness that we have avoided for three millennia. It has never flourished due to the inexorable remnants of the animal that create the stupour that forces our sentient awareness to remain in the subconscious. The closest thing to evil is the stupour in which we remain.

The lack of loving coitus is still the root cause of our troubles but the best interpretation of the damage, the first and foremost important victim is that in its absence, our desperate struggle to avoid the realization, crushed our sentient awareness for three millennia. We learned to lie and became an animal.

Sentient awareness is a rather unwieldy term that is hard to pin down at this time. Think of it as support for the group consciousness of our race, maybe. The group consciousness is becoming convinced we are no better than a miserable rutting animal reveling in the dark without the support of the clarity we attain when our sentient awareness is liberated. We remain split. Yes, it is the split personality that I have mentioned often. Either the animal or the human will win out in the long run.

It is not so easy to identify the human split, since it is not fully formed. But, the demented animal is hard to miss.

We have always touted humanity's intelligence. It is, of course, important. It is easy to see that as a clear difference between human and animal. It is also easy to implement. Big brain, big ideas, big actions, meaningless though they often are.

It is not the big difference that distinguishes between human and animal. Without the liberation of our sentient awareness, an honest perspective on what human life can be once we shed the animal, we remain a demented animal. It is time for win-win.

It is because intelligence is only a small part of the human picture, and the only part of the big picture that we have ever recognized, that we have failed as a sentient race.

What started it all was sentient awareness. Rather than root around doing what animals do, we realized there was more. Sentient awareness is all about dragging awareness out of the subconscious realm, in which it remains for animals, and looking it straight in the eye. We blinked when it comes to coitus.

It confounded us so severely as to make us look away. We closed our eyes and intentionally never opened them again. We became a race of liars that just look away from the true dilemma.

A good description of the subconscious is where we hide that which we can't handle. We can no longer shunt the most important aspect of existence into the subconscious and create lie after lie. Men *can* give. Men *can* love. Men *can* be human.

That makes us human. We will be able to look each other in the eye without any lies left in our hearts. Our hearts will have been educated. That would be true, even if men could not succeed at loving coitus. It would just be much more difficult to bring all of humanity around to a sane perspective.

The Prehuman condition versus the Human condition

Prehuman condition: "Everything is okay with the world as long as everything is okay in *my little* world. When something impinges on my consciousness that seems untoward, I will avoid it like the plague until it comes hammering home that it really can impinge on my life and lifestyle."

Like war, nuclear bombs, another plague, climate destruction so severe that we will intimately understand the phrase, "a frog in hot water" like never before - and much sooner than anyone admits. There are so many *man-made (prehuman-made)* disasters staring us in the face. But, everything is okay!!! "We don't care about humanity or the future. Just let me have today."

The *Human* condition reflects human *nature*. All of those grand, noble characteristics that we have mentioned for ages will finally begin to appear and take shape.

We will finally be able to find balance in our human existence.

I am not exactly sure how humanity will cope. I don't think it would be good to speculate too much. Reminds me of Arisians. Once the Level 3 humans came into being and had been trained up to a certain extent, the Arisians were smart enough to say, "It would be a mistake to lead you where we have not already been." The Level 3 human was far beyond the Arisian's potential. What? You don't read scifi??!?!

I'll just leave it as the balance between our intellect and our sentient awareness will have us acting like a human race. Within one hundred years of accepting the necessity of this change, we will be pulling *together* to get us out of the death spiral we are in. Maybe sooner, I hope. Another hundred years, the way we are headed, scares me spitless.

Prehuman condition: In a more general way, it might be said, "Aaah, whatever." Of course, many say, "I just want to lash out at this awful existence." Or, "let me create as much disruption and hate just for the fun of it". We do our best to ignore the prehuman condition. We don't ever look closely at the human because we are (wrongly) afraid of what we may find.

If it all ends, we only hope it ends after we die. For all the grand pronouncements about gods, most consider their death the end of existence. Most only really believe death. "Screw the world."

We spend our time perfecting toys and gadgets to distract humanity from the awful dilemma that has never been faced, causing all of the dilemmas we are not willing to face.

Human condition: Humanity will finally turn its eye on itself and seek improvement. Humanity will be seeking to perfect the human condition to match that of human *nature*. Don't let that confuse you. Human nature is a good thing.

If we make something, it will be important beyond filling someone's pocketbook and not caring whether it wrecks things too severely. A game of dodge ball with the stakes being humanity's ongoing viability will no longer be played.

That's going to have a whole lot to do with love, intellect, and precision thinking (the influence of a liberated sentient awareness).

I may be speaking out of turn here, but maybe we will find that rhoetry is helpful, maybe even as a language itself.

Sanity

Our sanity will be attained when we have nothing of moment left roaming around in our subconsciousness (assuming the subconscious doesn't just completely disappear).

The subconscious is an animal trait. It is where all of the thoughts that have manipulated us through fear are hidden away. It is where the animal roams and takes control. It is where revolutionary thoughts get stuck in an animal's brain.

The insanity of our situation is everywhere to be seen.

No one has been able to face that, in essence, everything about our current existence is insane. It is easier to label individuals as insane than admit that we are dismounted from our humanity. Stuff them full of pills and everything will be okay. Right.

Mindsets

The prehuman mindset is a perversion of the three musketeers slogan. "All for one and to hell with humanity, the human legacy and aspirations, and future generations." Or, "I am an awful person and I don't care. (since I can't learn to love)"

More and more, the woman is taking on these characteristics, as well as the male. That is a dire knell for humanity. The female was preset to her humanity. That the male is finally chipping it away completely is worrisome.

The overall movement is towards the demented animal. We progressed for a little while long ago (~three millennia), found the situation wanting without redress (i.e. loving coitus) and have been drowning in our delusions ever since.

Yes, after humanity has committed endless horrors, we may, once again, reel ourselves back in without finding our final balance. But, how many more times will we be able to do so?

How many more times will we test fate?

Future based on past

Yes, that is a double entendre.

Its meaning can be interpreted as the fact that we based our existence on the past of the animal. That is mostly what all of my books, so far, have been about.

But it also can be used in an attempt to explain our human future when we realize that everything we have ever done was based on a past of remaining an animal and becoming demented. In other words, once we shed the animal, what could happen? That is what I expect all of my future books, if any, to be about.

Maybe the easiest of those insights are all of the noble characteristics that we have incessantly failed to develop. They are real. They are screaming to be let free.

Future based on our humanity

I just reread *Millennium* (again) and I like it. The section on future think is problematic, at best. I can't say there is a lot there, other than hints. But, those hints are beginning to bear fruit.

Suffice it to say, I think I'm beginning to get a clearer image of where we *might* be headed, *if* we become human.

When one looks closely at the problems of our existence, it is *pre*humanity that causes our most onerous problems. Not nature, not the universe, not luck, voodoo, or tarot cards. It is us.

We look to fix things with laws and regulations. Those are no substitute for becoming human.

This And That
A personal view...

I just like these quotes so much I thought I would reiterate and maybe interpret or embellish a few. I think they are all informative. They drove me on.

"The smell of a world that is burned"
 - Jimi Hendrix

"Power at its most vicious is a riposte to powerlessness."
 - Simone de Beauvoir
    You may need to think this one through to get what I
    believe it means. To me, it is a comment on men.
    Simone knew what was going on.

""When will our consciences grow so tender that we will act to prevent human misery rather than avenge it?"
 - Eleanor Roosevelt (truly brilliant woman)
    My answer is easy. When we become human.

"Sure he (Fred Astaire) was great, but don't forget that Ginger Rogers did everything he did, ...backwards and in high heels."
 - Bob Thaves, "Frank and Ernest" comic strip; 'nuff said

"Darkness cannot drive out darkness; only light can do that.
Hate cannot drive out hate; only love can do that."
 - Martin Luther King, Jr.

"And nothing natural is evil"
  -Marcus Aurelius

"The unexamined life is not worth living"
"Let he that would move the world first move himself"
"From the deepest desires often come the deadliest hate"
  - Socrates
        A man that lived while sentience was in its heyday

"History is a pack of lies about events that never happened told by people who weren't there."
  - George Santayana
        I would add that history also obscures and redirects our attention away from what is important. Prehumanity concentrates on surface issues. it seeks excitement and distraction, not root cause.

"The reason why the world lacks unity, and lies broken and in heaps, is, because man is disunited with himself."
  -Ralph Waldo Emerson
        Essentially, this was the question that I asked myself throughout a lifetime. Like I said, one of my favorites.

"What lies behind you and what lies in front of you, pales in comparison to what lies inside of you."
  -Ralph Waldo Emerson
        He was right, again. Did he have any idea how right?

"And that's the thing
Do you recognize the bell of truth
When you hear it ring"

"I've got some words to say about the way we live today.
Why can't we learn to love each other.
It's time to learn a new face for the whole world wide human race."
  -Leon Russell

"For truth is always strange; stranger than fiction."
  -Lord Byron

"We are what we repeatedly do. Therefore, excellence is not an act, but a habit."
  -Aristotle

"A little learning is a dangerous thing
Drink deep, or taste not the Pierian Spring"
  -Alexander Pope, an impossible lesson for prehumanity

"There are only two ways to live your life. One is as though nothing is a miracle. The other is as though everything is a miracle."
— Albert Einstein

"It is never too late to be what you might have been."
— George Eliot
  Three thousand years seem late enough

"We accept the love we *think* we deserve."
— Stephen Chbosky
        Men are convinced they deserve hell.

"I saw ten thousand talkers whose tongues were all broken"
  -Bob Dylan

"One who asks a question feels like a fool for a moment. One who refuses to ask a question feels a fool for a lifetime." Or, a sentient race remains a fool for millennia.
  -Japanese proverb

Humanity remains a dilettante at sentience, a poser. We're on the threshold of something more, something truly human: sentient awareness. Something that can separate us decisively from the animal: loving coitus.

"This And That" is just short insights or comments that don't connect to each other in any particular way except as they reflect on loving coitus or sentient awareness in some way. I will *try* to minimize the self-revelations, repetitions, and speculation. They are separated by dash marks and an extra carriage return.

- It is all about graciousness that can only exist unimpeded in an environment that is consistent with a sentient reality, in which love is finally a major force.

- I have come to understand how difficult it is for people to grasp what I am explaining. That doesn't change much, really, just my perception of how difficult a task it is to reorient humanity into a loving race. It may take another.

- From very early on, I made a prediction of sorts. I suggested all that would initially change would be the tone of life. That life would become more ... smooth. That confidence and respect would begin to permeate our every step. That it would begin to be felt and seen in every human as the race finally began to gain confidence as it emerged from the long shadow of the animal.

I am more and more convinced this is exactly how it will play out. By the time tremendous changes begin to be wrought, we will be ready for them. Those changes, when they arrive, won't come as a surprise. We will be expecting them as our due.

Men and women walking side by side with a purpose, with a *shared* goal is subtle, only a change in tone, but tremendous.

I am also more and more convinced this will happen before any recognition of the change is voiced.

- It is becoming overwhelming to me as my eyes finally open and I begin to see the evidence all around.

I see it in every single love song ever written in the enthusiasm of youth. I see in the bitter dregs of love songs written in the miserable acceptance of the existing situation as the lyricist ages. I see it in the spurning of innocence.

I see it in the bitter actions of so many men and the sad acceptance in so many women.

I see it in paintings. The most striking to me is Degas' "In A Café". It describes so well the situation of both genders without a word. The man caught behind his mask of indifference and anger, never even really understanding what went wrong. The woman accepting her fate in misery.

The woman is all dressed up. Not because she is celebrating her life, her existence, her very essence, as she should. She is dressed up for her ~~man~~ male that wants to show off his *possession* that, at some point in the past, he really thought he would be able to love. His lack mystifies him. What happened? He becomes bitter. She becomes a possession in the depths of his selfishness.

Yeah, it is all all too clear.

- Humanity has attempted to attack its insanity from the outside inwards, from the minutia to the centerpiece. It has never even gotten close to detecting root cause of our demented state. It's never gotten beyond its inappropriate shame. Anytime we attempt to delve deeper, the distraction of the chaos of shame increases to make sure our attention is drawn away.

- This is the other part that I have been trying to stress. All of the perfidy, paranoia, and discombobulation that we endure is not the natural state of a fully sentient, human race. It is a travesty.

There is only one way that fits the sentient situation: accepting what our awareness makes clear.

Can you see how it has been more than difficult for me to provide an explanation *because* of all of the crap we have put in the way of ever exploring the concept of loving coitus?

The absence of acknowledgement of the lack of loving coitus is the root cause of all of our misery but it is not the most difficult to overcome. The most difficult is all that crap that developed due to our inability to acknowledge the situation for three thousand years.

- Let me cover some of the territory of our newly minted humanity that seems certain. If we ever acquire it.

First of all, finally, my heart's greatest desire. Equality and equitable circumstances for women seems assured.

Let me generalize another.

Humanity should finally rule rather than being witlessly ruled by inanities. Money being only one such.

- There's another point that I would like to clarify. I've talked about how the split personality, essentially, is the split between the practical and the dreamer. I've talked about how the two must merge for us to become truly human.

I've talked about how both 'sides' are right and both are wrong. This is the piece that I don't think I made as clear as I would like.

Our prehuman condition, our animal context, is why the split exists. It is why each can justify its position, even though both positions are so full of holes. Each position has something to point to and say, "You see! I'm right about this!" They are either accepting the animal's viewpoint or the human potential. Both are wrong *until* we become human. They never ever say anything about the holes the size of a cruise ship in their arguments. They just dig in their heels and take a stand. I'm about to throw up. The only reason I tend to side with the human potential is, well, the other side is just accepting the animal. It is not enough, though, to say, "we can be human" while remaining an animal. The stance is way too tentative for me.

- When will people get it through their heads it is the *prehuman state* that is misogynistic, driven by men failing to learn love! It is not individual, isolated events or men. Pointing at individual examples is just another example of "taking a stand" that does little until the whole is highlighted. Maybe it was the best that could be done, under the circumstances. It is similar to our stance on insanity. The prehuman race is insane, not individuals.

- Somehow, no one wants to believe that humanity can be sacred, glorified. As you read that sentence, there is a reasonable possibility that you will shudder in fear for your soul for even reading it. I did when I first began this journey. But, I could no longer tolerate the inanities that went with fictitious gods and the lies propounded by 'religious' individuals to cover their ass or presume advantage. The sanctimonious utterances began to make me ill.

We created gods because we don't want to admit that it all resides on our shoulders. It was dodging responsibility for our actions. It's very annoying, offensive, and wrong.

I will certainly be spinning in my grave if anyone calls me supernatural, *unless they include themselves and the rest of humanity in that definition*. My main quality? A deeply abiding honesty that forced the issue into the open, to my initial horror. My sentient awareness was more relentless than most.

- We are so used to our misery that I think most people think, when presented with the suggestion that men need to know how to perform well at coitus, that men should just buck up.

Why in the world should we tough it out? That is a dull-witted animal's solution for a race that is so far beyond the animal that it becomes demented attempting to remain an animal. It is hopeless to attempt to remain an animal with animal resolutions. It can't work. We can only be a demented, immensely destructive animal or become human.

It is a delusion because we have always believed there was no other option *because* we kept looking at it as an animal would.

What we should do, what we must do is transcend the animal and all of its baggage. Put away the gods and become human.

- There are no good choices until love flourishes. There is only one way that happens. This is the reason I spurned everything tainted with our prehumanity. Our prehumanity is not honest.

- The nice thing about this is there is no interpretation necessary. Unlike past attempts to make us more than a demented animal, this proves itself out through one agency: loving coitus.

You don't have to rely on a useless statement, like "Love is good" or "Peace is good". Of course they are good! The real question has always been how do we make them common. It is certainly *not* by howling at the top of our lungs about goodness.

There is no god proclaiming some foolishness from behind the clouds through the mouth of some aberrant human. I am utterly human. Physical loving is already upon us. Loving coitus is real, tangible, and right before us. All we have to do is try. The results can be nothing but good. The only question is how good.

Of course, it will take at least a few people learning that loving coitus can be attained. To me, they are the heroes. For the first few, it will take a tremendous effort of will to see it through.

This is nothing to create a mystic, nebulous, fictional, and useless god or religion about. There is nothing for some pompous asshole to use to his own advantage.

The physical aspect of love is all that matters. Loving coitus is the ultimate answer. It releases our humanity and enables our sentient awareness. No priest or priestess required.

We either learn to love through the agency of loving coitus or we don't. No matter what, we have to learn that mutual orgasm makes us human. Men either become something far more than the rutting brute animals that they have remained or they don't. Women finally attain the equality and equitable position that they deserve or they don't. It's all just a matter of honesty, really.

- I just can't get past my belief that coitus is different, special. It is not just that coitus makes babies. Sure, mutual orgasm, in any form is preferable to not. It certainly assures love to some extent. But, coitus is special. It is eye-to-eye love. It is the way we were built to provide the physical form of love.

Without loving coitus, I would be concerned. I am not sure an honest assessment of the situation without the advent of loving coitus could possibly fulfill us, though without it, that would be our only way forward. My guess is we would die out. We are already on that path, so nothing lost, if that were the case.

That still does not rule out other ways in which two people share physical love but coitus is the foundation without which I fear we never become fully human as a race of sentient beings.

I hate that I have to state it so carefully because of the reinforced positions of all of those that have had to find some other way to achieve love. I give them kudos for seeking love in whatever form they could. It is entirely possible that the other forms of physical love will continue, even once loving coitus becomes common. There may be other factors involved.

The biggest difference, if they do, in the presence of loving coitus, is that there won't be any concern. It is only the lack of viable loving coitus that makes so many heterosexuals insane when contemplating a form of sex that includes shared orgasm.

In this particular case, loving coitus is not a necessity. If all heterosexuals were to find some way in which to provide mutual orgasm, the plight of alternatives would still disappear.

Still, coitus is special. It is elegant, natural. It is human, once we make it so. Any animal can perform any other form of sex.

- It's pretty clear now. We are barreling in the direction of our sentience. While I really believe I revealed the key piece, I'm fairly certain, like so many grand discoveries, it will get here soon, even without anyone reading my writings. Considering I am averse to making a big noise, that may be a good thing.

- As far as I can tell, those that have read my books are thoroughly dumbstruck. Just like I was. At least, I hope so.

Just like me, they should get over it. What is amazing is just how simple it will be for the prehuman to become human. What is more amazing still is how difficult it is to convince the human animal that it can easily become a wholesome human sentient race.

It's just that all of those paradigms of nonsense bearing down on the poor animal leaves so little room for the prehuman to maneuver.

- It was due to rhoetry that I was able to uncover this anomaly in our existence. I know, I said I'd stay off of personal subjects but I believe this could be important.

There is something about rhoetry. I say that it allows me to look right while gazing left, or that it allows me to see around corners. I get so caught up in providing for the rhyme and rhythm that my mind becomes free to explore the subconscious. I really believe there will be little left in the subconscious so, maybe seeing around corners won't be important once we gain our humanity.

As I wrote all of these seven books, I have groaned that I could not write rhoetry to convey the same message. It is my language of choice. I despised prose. I still do. Rearranging my mind in such a way to write passable prose was painful.

There is no beauty.

As I wrote this book on the subject, I realized that I need to rearrange further. I need to bring the same elegance, that was natural for me in rhoetry, to the fore. It is strange to me to think of prose as elegant. All I can do is try. I don't expect success.

With rhoetry, it often began with the appropriate title. Once that was done, the writing itself flowed out of me. After writing this once through thoroughly, I have the title. Now, I will just have to go back and rewrite the book right on through, once more. I hope that the elegance approaches that of rhoetry.

I do see many signs that what I am saying is catching on. But, they are so minimal, so understated, that it doesn't inspire me to a great deal of hope. It just breaks my heart. Sometimes, that feels like what this life has been all about. I guess one could say that is what our existence has been all about up until this point. Broken hearts.

The Heart Of Corruption

Of course, the title is a double-entendre. I am attempting, here, to lay as plain as possible what happened to corrupt men's hearts. I don't know. Maybe I already explained it well enough. Since it hasn't gone viral, how should I know?

I will try to describe the historical process by which men became completely corrupted to the existence of an animal over the millennia and how they become corrupted over a lifetime.

It is the corruption process that each man goes through as well as the true story of our history. It is a consensus that started millennia ago. It has to do with that which bends their brains back upon itself, ruining any chance of attaining their sentient awareness and becoming human until they learn to love in bed.

To some extent, the failure has always been known. I still wonder if the animals are aware. It has just become more apparent with each passing day of the history of humanity as our relentless awareness continues to bang away at the door.

As we continued to hide the truth, we have become more adept at lying and destruction.

When one thinks of an animal realizing its failure, it makes one wonder. It almost makes sense. Is it just a matter of articulation? Is our fear of articulating the failure tied more directly to the animal than I have suggested? Did the animal always know? Was the prevention of our articulation predestined? It just makes a lot of sense if the animal always knew. Did we grow up amidst the unconscious awareness of failure? Did the acceptance of the belief that it must fail predate us?

As history progressed, it became easier and easier for men to become corrupted to their very souls as the realization of failure became more and more apparent and the deceits, obfuscation, and violence grew as a distraction from that realization.

You want a devil to blame all suffering on? Well, there it is.

After a rather short span of time in the distant past, men were conditioned further and further, from the time of birth with convincing arguments that things were just as they should be - since they hadn't figure out that humanity should attain a much more delightful existence and were at a loss to make loving coitus work *in a natural manner* (yeah, still emphasizing pills are worse than useless. They are our failure lit bright). Men became fully deluded that they could not overcome the obstacle that animals had endured for a billion years. Their powers of intellect were not enough alone to break the barrier early on in our existence.

There was little intellect, just babbling mouths. Exactly, things haven't change much at all.

Ummm, I think I got derailed but I think this passage helps, still.

The following paragraph is for the advanced student of our humanity to put together. But, I want to paint this in broad brushstrokes that anyone with an open mind can easily follow.

Since the moment we began to skew away from our humanity because men became convinced that they had to pull the wool over the eyes of all of humanity rather than articulate something that was lacking in their stature, it has been pulling humanity apart. That is not a metaphor.

- I thought it would also be a good idea to generalize the two genders' perspectives, as well.

It is not nearly so starkly black and white as I often seem to portray it.

There are good men and there are bad women. I think that confuses a lot of people. Just as I say that I had to look at humanity as a single entity to even begin to comprehend what was going on, I had to do the same with the genders.

While there are good and bad behaviours of both genders, one has to look past the "good" and "bad" to the origin, commonality, and intensity of the behaviour in each genders, as well as the history of the two genders. One also has to look past the excuses we have accepted for each to the deeper truth.

I mentioned the best depiction I have seen of the two genders was in a painting by Edgar Degas. What really staggered me as I awoke today with a pristine smile on my face for the first time in about sixty years was the idea that a very, very, very few men have woken with that smile on their faces over the millennia.

I'm feeling pretty good. I've been so involved in strategy all of my life that I *know* a few key things that will let me rest in my grave with some level of satisfaction.

The history of strategic thinking makes me certain that, no matter what I do, it will take a long while to grasp what I am saying and for humanity to begin to do something about it in a big way. If I were much more of a mountebank, a seeker of unbridled attention, maybe it would be different. But not mountebank could have sustained the necessary effort, much less the necessary honesty.

No matter what I do, prehumanity will fight its ascension into its humanity. Almost certainly, I will not be around to see it become a human certainty. I will not see it become part of the Great Conversation. Not exactly satisfying but comforting to know well how strategic changes evolve.

Secondly, I *know* I did quite a job of spreading its awareness to a lot of folks. Thus, I can go to my grave with a fair confidence that it will take hold at some point and, at least, the comfort of knowing that the knowledge is out there, whether it comes to fruition or not. I just can't believe that the stupour is that deep.

There is also the other point I mentioned. The groundswell actually started long ago. If we survive, we will get there, sooner or later.

Fate sure picked the wrong person to whom to reveal this. I feel like the worst guide ever. As I said, explanations just don't seem to be my forte. Understanding is my forte. Maybe that is the only way it could be, at least at this point in time. Maybe there is one last push that will be required. No, it won't be me.

I have said after every book that I am finished. I will not do so this time. I am elated. I think I've put it in terms that some should be able to comprehend. I believe, in this book, I have dodged the millions of nonsense paradigms that have developed over past millennia that cause everyone to look away or justify their bizarre take on the animal we remain. Of course, that does not mean I am going to get through to anyone, just a chance.

Finally, I realized there are just two ways I finish. Either I find a way to penetrate the stupour of prehumanity or I die.

I've come up with another term that may be helpful if humanity decides to explore further. Post-animal. Maybe the best way to describe our situation for most of the past three millennia is post-animal. It may be best to only consider the last century or so as prehuman. Maybe dating it as beginning around the time of the Flower Power generation would be best.

I finally realized something. Most sensitive people like me convince themselves that they are not suited for this world. In one way or another, they divorce themselves from the world. I am way more determined than that and far more confident of myself. I have always been convinced that this world, as is, isn't suited for me. Only one course, in that case. Get to the bottom of why this world isn't suitable for a human. I have done so.

I may even get back to writing rhoetry. The rhoetry that I adore. The rhoetry is all about the beauty of this existence without the demented influence of the animal. It also makes clear why I adore one woman so much. She sees the beauty, like no other. The reason it breaks my heart is that she understands the demented, also. That is what alway drove me on. I needed to make precision clear that the demented state need not exist. Maybe she'll see it in this lifetime or maybe she won't. Either is okay. I just had to make it clear. That same stubborn streak.

I finally mastered our predicament in all of its complexity.

- I saved this for last because it is new, so tentative. I've harped on laws and how we attempt to restrict the 'bad habits' of the animal, which never really addressed the natural desire to be human. But, this put it in a new light.

As with so much of this journey, this was *another* level that needed to be broached. This is why it has taken me seven books to get this far in understanding.

I save it for last because it has not been tested, rung out thoroughly. Like the rest, it is right. It just may not be worded as well as another seven books could make it.

It is just a matter of removing the blinders. We are almost there.

Do you get it? We have been chasing the bad behaviour like it is some sort of disease that just needs to be controlled. More laws, more limitations, more restrictions, more excuses for pompous behaviour. For the animal, there will always be more laws. For the human, I am beginning to think that laws will be completely frivolous.

Maybe laws and what they address are all just symptoms of a disturbed state of sentience. Look at the headlines. We make a big deal out of identifying specific incidences of our inability to put away the animal. I was just reading: "homophobic behaviour is more common than you thought" or "Museum closes racist, sexist, ableist display". None of it changes anything. It's like saying, "We are horrible. Just look!" What in the world is that supposed to accomplish? Laws are similar. Once we are truly human, will there be any need for any laws?

It is surrender to the animal. As if we couldn't expect to do any better. Do you yet recognize the defeatist?

The real question is not a matter of what is the next monstrosity. There is no categorical list of monstrosities because, as long as we remain a demented animal, some monstrosity will crop up in some new form. It's not a matter of keeping ourselves on our toes to discover the next monstrosity or the repeat of one as old as humanity (which is the usual case). The question is what causes all of the monstrosities?

Humanity's reaction to laws tells you what you need to know. The reaction brought on by allowing the animal to remain in charge is that everyone seeks a way around the laws.

Do you see the problem? We aren't improving humanity by any number of laws. There is always another law, ad infinitum, as long as the animal attempts to find ways around the laws.

We aren't becoming more human. We just further restrict the animal that should be long gone in the first place.

We could be human.

While I tried to broaden the scope of this book to take into account the possibility that coitus does not become a loving event, I do not believe it. I do not believe that coitus cannot become a natural, unassisted loving event. I am convinced that, if anyone *tries*, they will find not only that they can do so, it will be easy, once attained. As I have said repeatedly, as future generations arrive bearing the confidence of the former generation, they will wonder what took us so long.

I also do not believe there is any other answer. If worse comes to worst, we will have to try. In my case, just give me a bullet for the brain. *Loving* coitus is meant to be available for all.

The lack of love, the lack of giving in an intimate relationship in the most natural manner possible, leaves a gaping hole in the male psyche that grows and grows from the time they reach puberty and discover they are not yet human. That cannot change until loving coitus becomes human.

Thank you for reading this book
whickwithy@gmail.com

www.ingramcontent.com/pod-product-compliance
Lightning Source LLC
Chambersburg PA
CBHW050545280326
41933CB00011B/1733